# Table of Contents

# Foreword

Data-driven, or data-based, decision making has been an essential part of school improvement efforts for some time, but we have seen important changes in the process during the past few years. These changes affect how data are understood, collected, and applied to instructional and programmatic decisions at all levels. For school leaders facing the ever-increasing challenges of changing student demographics, accompanied by state and federal accountability requirements, effective use of data can be critical to the success of school improvement efforts. And classroom assessments have taken on new urgency with the advent of the Response to Intervention (RTI) approach.

Principals need to understand what this wealth of data means and how to use it in positive and productive ways in order to be truly effective as school leaders. The second edition of *Data-Based Decision Making*, addresses this need. It presents both research and practical experience in a down-to-earth discussion of what every school leader should know about the topic. This edition includes information on the preconditions for effective data use, suggests approaches to developing a system of data use in your school, and highlights ways to use data to support improvement.

Each publication in the *Essentials for Principals* series is jointly developed by the National Association of Elementary School Principals (NAESP) and Educational Research Service (ERS) to provide information that is both practical and solidly grounded in research on issues of vital importance to school leaders. This publication, the first in the updated *Essentials* series, is a valuable resource for both beginning and experienced principals. Each book in this series provides principals with tools and resources that are integral in meeting the NAESP standards outlined in the second edition of *Leading Learning Communities: Standards for What Principals Should Know and Be Able To Do*. This edition of *Data-Based Decision Making* specifically addresses Standard 5, "manage data and knowledge to inform decisions and measure progress of student, adult, and school performance."

NAESP and ERS believe that this *Essentials* guide will help principals provide the best possible leadership on using data to improve their schools and promote high levels of student learning.

Gail Connelly
*Executive Director*
National Association of Elementary
School Principals

Katherine A. Behrens
*Acting President and Chief Operating Officer*
Educational Research Service

# Chapter 1
# Introduction

*"Data-driven decision making.... It reminds practitioners that their plans have a greater likelihood of succeeding if the goals and strategies within them are based on solid information and not on hunches or habit"* (Center for Comprehensive School Reform and Improvement, 2006, p. 1).

The phrase "data for decision making" has been used so often in discussions of school improvement efforts that it has become almost a mantra. In general, that's a good thing. Effective use of data has been repeatedly tied to successful efforts to increase levels of student achievement. But the word effective should be stressed. It's *how* educators use data that really provides the critical link between practice and school improvement.

The "how" of data-based decision making has changed over the past few years. Educators have become more sophisticated in their use of data. In part, this is due to increased availability of user-friendly data that supports principals' and teachers' use of information about student achievement. The increased emphasis on data use also brought with it more training and heightened educators' awareness of how data use can help diagnose problems and identify possible solutions. So what we're seeing today in many schools is an increase in the use of data, the types of data used, and the number of ways data are used.

Knapp, Swinnerton, Copland, and Monpas-Huber discuss this evolution in the use of data:

> An argument can be made that educational leaders have always had "data" of some kind available to them when making decisions intended to improve teaching and learning. Effective leaders gathered whatever information they could readily access, and then drawing on accumulated experience, intuition, and political acumen, they chose the wisest course of action to pursue. The data

they collected was likely impressionistic and rarely systematic, complete, or sufficiently nuanced to carry the weight of important decisions (2007, p. 2).

They go on to describe a more thoughtful and intentional approach to using data and call this "data-informed leadership" (p. 5). This phrase has important implications for principals since providing the leadership to encourage effective data use in their schools is emerging as one of their most important responsibilities. Knapp, Swinnerton, Copland, and Monpas-Huber also stress that this change in terminology away from data-driven decision making signals an important shift in the way data use should be viewed. In this new framework, data are not thought to "drive" decisions. Instead, data use acknowledges that educators bring into the process:

> …core values and insights into those aspects of the practice for which there are not yet good data, and may never be…. The notion of data-informed leadership captures the complex and often ambiguous nature of data use in educational settings (p. 6).

This notion of data also stresses that an important outcome of data analysis should be to "prompt questions and deliberations" (Knapp et al., 2007, p. 6). Obviously, principals will need to play a key role in developing a school culture that supports this more intensive—and often less obvious—use of data. Creighton describes it this way: "We must become more proactive and move beyond the 'on the surface' work with data—and investigate 'below the surface' issues related to our data" (2007, p. 1-2).

---

*"Data can and should be used as a mechanism for having conversations about school processes, direction, results, capacity, and improvement…. Data becomes information, and information becomes knowledge when people make sense out of it through thoughtful conversations that shape the information to make it meaningful in their context. This gives them the foundation for making wise decisions based on their new knowledge"* (Earl & Katz, 2008, p. 8).

---

Killion and Bellamy also stress the importance of data to school improvement. They suggest that "because data abound, schools must become data savvy":

> Without analyzing and discussing data, schools are unlikely to identify and solve the problems that need attention, identify appropriate interventions to solve those problems, or know how they are progressing toward achievement of their goals. Data are the fuel of reform.... In short, using data separates good schools from mediocre schools. Schools that are increasing student achievement, staff productivity and collegiality, and customer satisfaction use data to inform and guide their decisions and actions. Data use essentially sets a course of action and keeps a staff on that course to school improvement and student success (2000).

Aldersebaes, Potter, and Hamilton speak of "using data to ignite change" (2000, p. 20), with school staff using "meaningful" data to:

- uncover needs, priorities, and resources;
- build a school profile to better understand the school's strengths and weaknesses;
- develop intrinsic motivation through identifying a need for change;
- create a focused direction for change accompanied by realistic goals; and
- establish a baseline against which to measure progress and design a plan to evaluate programs or practices.

The bottom line—it makes sense to use data to help clarify decisions, identify alternative solutions to problems, and target resources more effectively. The real question should not be *whether* to integrate the use of data in school improvement, but *how*. However, identifying good data and using it effectively is obviously a complex process, one that many schools are just beginning to address.

This *Essentials for Principals* is designed to help principals become more knowledgeable about using data in their leadership responsibilities. The how-to's of building a school culture in which data use is seen as a natural and necessary part of a process of continuous improvement will be discussed. One aspect of this development will be addressing important preconditions, such as staff education in data use. Another is putting in place some of the nuts and bolts of effective data use.

The discussion will then turn to several ways principals, teachers, and other staff members can develop and use data to support improvement of instruction and other school functions. Each of these chapters is organized around three commonsense, practical questions:

- What are you looking for?
- How will you look for it?
- How will you use the data?

Embedded throughout this book are references to the important role principals play in moving their school toward effective data use. You will need to provide support for the process and demonstrate your commitment to use of data in decision making. We hope the content provided here will give you the information you need to do this well.

# Chapter 2
# Preconditions for Effective Data Use

*"One thing is crystal clear from the research to date: where it occurs, data-informed leadership is a direct reflection of aggressive, persistent attempts by leaders to create conditions in which this way of approaching the business of schooling can flourish"* (Knapp, Swinnerton, Copland, & Monpas-Huber, 2007, p. 37).

Thornton and Perreault talk about "necessary prior conditions" for successful data-based leadership. In their view,

> These conditions include a shared vision, a trust-filled environment, and a principal who understands data. If these are not present within the school, then it is essential that they be developed before proceeding, because their absence will significantly undermine any data-based efforts to improve the school (2002, p. 87).

Principal leadership is embedded in ensuring "prior conditions" are present. However, there are other ways in which a principal can develop an environment supportive of data use. Thornton and Perreault talk about this:

> Demonstrating the utility of data is critical to gaining teachers' support and cooperation. In general, teachers need to become comfortable consumers; the data collected should become 'their' data…. By engaging staff members in a meaningful project, the principal can identify and model the value of data-based decision making….To build teachers' confidence in data analysis, the principal should select an initial project that is likely to succeed (2002, p. 90).

Holcomb (2004) identifies some barriers to data use she has observed in her work with educators. These barriers include:

- lack of training—including time to practice with use of the data as well as skill acquisition
- lack of time—specifically time to work collaboratively
- feast or famine—the sense in the beginning that needed data are not available, often followed by the feeling of being swamped with data
- fear of evaluation
- fear of exposure since work with data often moves people out of their comfort zones
- Confusing a technical problem with a cultural problem—specifically, effective data analysis requires "accepting collective responsibility for the learning of students" (p. 32) in addition to number crunching.

Explicitly addressing these barriers can help to provide more fertile ground for the growth of data-based decision making. Johnson (2002) suggests including self-reflection in your planning. For example, "What do you perceive as your major issues and roadblocks around engaging in data use?" "What strengths do you bring to the table around data use?" "What kinds of professional development do you need to become a more effective user of data?"

Now, let's move ahead to discussing some of the essential preconditions for effective schoolwide data use.

## A Trusting Environment

It's easy to see why some staff members might fear increased use of data since it can shine a brighter light on school problems or—even more worrisome—on their lack of success with some students. Thus, your role as principal in developing a trusting environment needs to begin long before you increase your emphasis on data use.

As an example of the importance of trust to data use, Langer, Colton, and Goff talk about a group of teachers engaged in collaborative analysis of student work: "Trust in fellow group members allows you to bring a struggling student's work to the group without fear of being judged or criticized" (2003, p. 46).

## Training for Staff

Clearly, teachers and other staff members will need support—especially training—in how to address these important functions. This element has been addressed head-on by schools that have incorporated the effective use of data in their improvement efforts. Opportunities to learn how to analyze assessment data have typically been provided in a variety of ways, including:

- staff development focused on how to "read" and analyze reports of assessment results;
- presentations by central office staff or principals to school staff, followed by a discussion of possible next steps;
- one-on-one sessions of a principal, assistant principal, or lead teacher with a teacher to review and discuss results from their classes and students; and
- training of an in-school data expert, typically a teacher, who works with grade-level or subject-area teams to analyze the data.

However, Holcomb reminds us that effective data use requires more than number-crunching skills. For this reason,

> The ability, capacity, and commitment to use data cannot be developed through training in the traditional sense of courses and workshops. It is far more complex than individual knowledge and skill acquisition, and it must be embedded in the ongoing work of groups of professionals (2004, p. 30).

Thus, training is often especially powerful when it is organized around an "authentic" task. For example, when teachers are carefully supported through their initial efforts to use assessment data to improve classroom instruction, they are simultaneously learning important skills. Reeves talks about a process that could fill this dual purpose role of data use and training:

- Have faculty agree on the "12 most important standards for each subject, each grade." The way to accelerate is to have teachers answer this question: "What knowledge and skills do students need in the next lower grade in order to come into your class with confidence and success next year?" Whereas fifth grade teachers may not narrow the focus for themselves, they have little trouble in narrowing the focus for fourth grade.

- Have faculty teams design very short assessments that, over the course of a year, address these brief sets of power standards. "Very short" means about 15 items, 12 multiple choice, and 3 extended response. This should not take more than 20 minutes of classroom time each month, and the grading can be immediate.

- Provide some time in faculty meetings or already scheduled group time to grade the three quick extended response items. Insure that the credit given is consistent—that is, faculty members can look at an anonymous piece of student work and agree on whether it is "proficient" and what credit it should receive.

- Provide time in faculty meetings after each assessment has been graded to get very clear answers to this question: Based on the results we have just observed, how will the next few weeks and months be different in schedule, curriculum, and teaching strategies? (2004).

Finally, training for staff should include time spent on encouraging teachers and other school staff to recognize the data analysis skills they already have. Earl and Katz talk directly to educators who feel they "cannot do this 'data stuff' because they are no good with math." They stress that "data literacy is not the same as 'crunching numbers'" (2006, p. 45) and go on to describe what they mean by data literacy. It is a thinking process—a process of:

- standing back and deciding what you need to know and why,
- collecting or locating the necessary data,
- finding ways to link key data sources, ensuring that the data are worth considering,
- being aware of their limitations,

- thinking about what the results mean, and finally,
- systematically considering an issue from a range of perspectives so that you really feel that you have evidence to explain, support, and also challenge your point of view (2006, p. 45).

For principals, learning how to analyze and use the data often requires aligning this knowledge with other supervisory skills. For example, a principal interviewed by Cromey and Hanson reported using assessment data to:

identify, then intervene with teachers whose students consistently performed lower on a variety of assessments compared to other teachers. The principal indicated that these data neutralize potentially daunting conversations by providing objective information that can be further probed to identify more specific instructional needs. Further, attempts by the teacher to improve his or her teaching can be evaluated with the same data. The principal acknowledged that many teachers have had negative experiences when using student data because they have been "hit over the head with it." Therefore, the principal used data constructively and attempted to frame these conversations proactively (2000).

> *"Colleagues sitting down to look at and discuss student work . . . are practicing an essential form of assessment data collection"* (Gregory & Kuzmich, 2004, p. 69).

## Opportunities for Teachers to Collaborate

Another key component of effective systems is the provision of time for teachers to discuss the data and to work together to develop solutions. Teachers view this time as an opportunity both to develop their skills in data analysis and to brainstorm and share effective instructional strategies. While common planning time is often difficult to provide, Cromey and Hanson describe systems used in four schools they visited (see Table 2.1).

**Table 2.1.  Scheduling Approaches for Teacher Collaboration**

| | School A | School B | School C | School D |
|---|---|---|---|---|
| **Time and Planning Strategies** | Once every month, the school day begins two hours later—teachers meet during this time to engage in the activities described below. School makes up this accumulated time by extending the school year. | School staff are released early from school once per week for at least 45 minutes. This time is added to other days throughout the week.<br><br>Entire staff meets once a week for one hour before school. Staff decreased the "nuts and bolts" of the meetings and prioritized work related to assessment. | Same-grade teachers meet informally during weekly planning periods and formally every six weeks. To accommodate these planning periods, students in entire grades are sent to "specials" (e.g., gym, art classes). Time is also allotted at regularly scheduled staff meetings.<br><br>Teachers are released from teaching duties several days each year and are replaced by substitute teachers.<br><br>Teachers meet with the principal up to three times each year. | Teachers request time to meet with each other during school hours; substitutes are hired to support this. In addition, teachers meet after school.<br><br>Teachers meet in "within-grade" and "subject-area" teams during their planning hours once per week. |
| **Activities** | School staff rewrite district standards and realign the assessments they use accordingly.<br><br>School staff continuously re-evaluate this work, and discuss and plan changes as needed. | School staff use allotted time to align curriculum across grades and with the state standards. This process is driven by student assessment data.<br><br>School staff continuously re-evaluate this work and discuss and plan changes as needed. | Staff discuss students' progress according to the "developmental continuums" written by school staff.<br><br>Teachers administer individual assessments to students.<br><br>Staff discuss reports on assessment data from the district research department. | Staff share knowledge gained from professional development activities that addressed curriculum and assessment. They also discuss student mastery of standards and other outcomes and possible intervention strategies. |

Source: Cromey and Hanson (2000)

> *"For practitioners to develop a commitment to data use…school cultures that trust data and support high-quality data use must be nurtured"* (Heritage & Yeagley, 2005, p. 334).

## Developing a Culture of Data Use

Principals who want to build a culture of data use in their schools must look first to themselves. Ask yourself, am I demonstrating use of data in making decisions—or do staff members only hear me talking about the importance of using it? You should be modeling use of data every day.

One challenge to principals working to build a schoolwide program of data use may be breaking down the closed-door culture of teaching. Boudett and Moody talk about the importance of making data study a collaborative approach from the very beginning:

> Even in cases where one person is willing to assume primary responsibility for data work, it is important that that person not work alone. Assembling a group of people, assigning responsibility for specific tasks, and planning how individuals will coordinate their efforts with each other and the rest of the school sends a message that using data in your school will be a collaborative effort (2005, p. 14).

Finally, the relationship of school culture and data use often is a two-way process. As teachers learn to use data, it not only becomes second nature, it begins to affect other aspects of their teaching in a positive way:

> In learning to incorporate data analysis as a regular part of their professional activity, teachers become more reflective about their teaching practices, less reactive, less willing to accept easy answers, and more open-minded to solutions based on the data they gather (Wade, 2001, p. 2).

# Notes, Reminders, and Ideas:

_____

_____

_____

_____

_____

_____

_____

_____

_____

_____

_____

_____

_____

_____

_____

_____

_____

_____

_____

_____

_____

_____

_____

_____

# Chapter 3
# Developing a Process

Some schools are already sophisticated data users. They have developed approaches that work for them—yielding good information and making effective use of staff time. However, many others want to increase data use and want to move forward without stumbling. Gregory and Kuzmich suggest that more successful approaches often start small. For example, they "limit [the] focus, and spend time dialoguing about what works and for which students" (2004, p. 192). City, Kagle, and Teoh suggest that principals working to establish a more comprehensive approach to data use in their schools first ask themselves:

> How much time do you have to collect and analyze the data? What other resources do you have available to you? The answers to these questions influence how many data sources you can examine and which ones you choose (2005, p. 113).

Mike Schmoker agrees and provides some concrete suggestions for a school that wants to begin using assessment data to improve instruction:

> Concentrate on three very simple things—focused, collaborative learning; measurable goals; and data. Begin by looking at the data to establish one or two measurable goals. Have teachers get together in the summer when they have time and can be more relaxed to select or create periodic assessments by which they will measure progress related to that goal. Then have teams of teachers get together regularly to talk about their progress, focusing like a laser beam on specific emergent problems preventing students from doing well relative to that year-end goal. If a school does these things, it is all but certain to make some real progress (Sparks, 2000).

Johnson suggests that "a logical first step in using data is to begin making better use of existing data. A systematic analysis of data that are already being collected can reveal previously unseen patterns and opportunities for improvement" (2000). Depka has another suggestion in regard to data use and advises principals to guard against a "the more, the merrier" approach to data use:

> Be selective about the data you choose . . . The data you select should relate to your goal. If the plan is to analyze student academic achievement, choose the sources that will give you the best all-around indications. It is important to provide enough data so that participants can have a good degree of confidence that their observations are accurate. Too much information at one data delve can overwhelm, confuse, and exhaust people. There is certainly a time and place to view it all, but the data should be viewed in segments to avoid data overload (2006, p. 22).

Keeping the very real constraints of time—especially teacher time—in mind is obviously important. Thus, while some approaches to data collection and analysis may, by their nature, require fairly intensive investments of time, other approaches can be easy to implement while providing helpful data. For example, Depka suggests that teachers use color-coding when recording low scores in a grade book. The use of the different color "creates a visual of those in need of occasional support and identifies students who are experiencing repeated difficulties" (2006, p. 69). This visual could be helpful to the teacher when planning instruction and can also provide data for teacher-principal meetings on student progress or a discussion among teachers working to identify additional strategies to use with students having difficulty.

Finally, City, Kagle, and Teoh also talk about trade-offs principals need to consider as they begin schoolwide data use initiatives:

> If you examine instruction more quickly with limited data sources, you will get to designing and implementing solutions faster, but you may sacrifice some accuracy in understanding the teaching dimensions of the problem of

practice. If you take your time and examine several data sources, you may be more accurate, but you may lose a sense of urgency and momentum for improvement…. If you have a few people do most of the examining instruction work, you may get it done more quickly and at greater depth, but you may not get the level of understanding and buy-in you'll want from the rest of the teachers whose practice you ultimately want to improve (2005, p. 114).

> *"Researchers studying schools and other workplaces have found that leaders who are most successful at transforming their organizations are those who know how to frame important questions and then engage their colleagues in finding creative answers"* (Boudett & Steele, 2007, p. 2).

Ultimately, your goal should be to embed the use of data in the day-to-day operations of your school and as part of a continuous cycle of school improvement. Depka talks about this:

> For data analysis to ultimately have an impact on student achievement, it needs to be part of a cyclical process. When data analysis is viewed as one step in a system, its use will become integral to the workings of an organization. Without a process, data analysis can be only an event. Time is spent viewing and analyzing data, but there is no intended result other than to comment on what is observed. Although time is not wasted, data viewed without a process will not likely become a catalyst for change (2006, p. 2).

Thornton and Perreault agree and describe the alignment of data use with a cycle of school improvement. Note how data collection and use are embedded in their description of the cycle:

- **Develop a plan.** The plan should focus data collection efforts on a specific systemic issue or issues. What data will be collected? How will we improve the system? What new instructional methods or procedure will be developed? What is the current baseline on critical measures? What staff development is needed?

- **Implement the plan.** Did we successfully implement the plan? How well is the plan working? Do staff members need further professional development? Regular assessments should be conducted. At this stage, it is crucial to monitor implementation, collect data, and provide feedback.
- **Analyze the results.** Are staff members working collaboratively? Are staff members exhibiting skills and confidence in data analysis…. When determining whether the implementation is successful, criteria to consider are disaggregation of data, performance-based summaries, and open discussions.
- **Take action.** What have we learned? How can we improve the system? What adjustments in the system do the data suggest? (excerpted from Thornton & Perreault, 2002, p. 92-93).

# Notes, Reminders, and Ideas:

_____

_____

_____

_____

_____

_____

_____

_____

_____

_____

_____

_____

_____

_____

_____

_____

_____

_____

_____

_____

_____

_____

_____

_____

# Notes, Reminders, and Ideas:

_____

_____

_____

_____

_____

_____

_____

_____

_____

_____

_____

_____

_____

_____

_____

_____

_____

_____

_____

_____

_____

_____

_____

_____

# Chapter 4
# Using Assessment Data to Improve Instruction

*What are you looking for?*
*How will you look for it?*
*How will you use the data?*

---

*"Assessment is the process of gathering information about children from several forms of evidence, then organizing and interpreting that information"* (McAfee, Leong, & Bodrova, 2004, p. 3).

---

Although much of the current emphasis on using assessment data began with data from high-stakes tests, schools that are the most effective users of assessment data have begun to recognize and capitalize on the power of classroom assessment. Damian urges teachers and school leaders to embed assessment in "every aspect of our planning, thinking, and doing" instead of viewing assessment as a "once-a-year crisis" (2000, p. 16). Gregory and Kuzmich talk about this more comprehensive approach:

> High-stakes test data gives us only one piece of evidence about student learning. Well-designed classroom data collection and analysis, the everyday information a teacher collects, form the backbone of student growth…. Effective use of classroom data increases the probability that more students will demonstrate proficient and higher levels of performance (2004, p. 9-10).

They go on to talk about diagnostic teaching, an approach built around data use. In their view, diagnostic teaching moves past simply assessing to gauge progress—or lack of it. Instead, "true diagnostic thinking requires teachers to reflect consciously on student learning and then connect their conclusions to the most effective next steps" (2004, p. 52). Teachers using this type diagnosis as a tool to improve their teaching collect data that allow them to answer these questions:

- What do I know about my students now?
- What is the nature and content of the final assessment for this unit or period of time?
- What don't I know about the content knowledge, the critical thinking, and the process or skill demonstration of my students? (2004, p. 56).

Creating appropriate assessments and then using the data they produce takes time, time teachers often view as taken from instructional time they are reluctant to give up. Assessment, however, should be considered part of the teaching process and when used effectively, can make teaching more productive and time-efficient. Recognizing this, effective teachers incorporate assessment opportunities into their lesson planning (Aschbacher, Koency, & Schacter, 1995).

## An Assessment Framework

The heart of assessment is a continuing process in which both teachers and students use information to guide the next steps in learning. For the student, assessment provides feedback on understanding. Results of a test or comments on a written assignment will help him or her answer questions such as, "Am I getting it?" and, "How am I doing?" Assessments can help teachers answer related questions such as, "Which students are learning?" Similarly, an analysis of the results can help a teacher pinpoint specific difficulties or misconceptions to further explain or correct. Teachers can also use assessments for diagnostic purposes. When applied to the class, the data can answer such questions as, "Is the class ready for a new unit?" Reviewing assessment information for an individual student helps a teacher decide who needs additional help—and what type of help—as well as who can move on.

There are specific characteristics that tell us that assessment is being effectively used to guide instruction in the classroom:

- Assessment is embedded and ongoing and provides prompt, user-friendly feedback so adjustments can be made as needed, not just reported at the end of each learning-improvement cycle.
- Day-to-day classroom assessments emphasize formative assessments—information that provides early indication of whether or not learning is taking place—to minimize problems that might arise if learning barriers are not promptly identified and addressed.
- Day-to-day classroom assessments include qualitative data such as information from classroom observation as well as quantitative measures.
- Students are told the purpose of an assessment and how this information will be used.

Niyogi highlights some elements of high-quality, classroom-based assessment that make it a potentially powerful tool:

> Assessment should be used not simply to judge how much kids know but to illuminate the nature of their knowledge and understandings in order to help kids learn…. Common sense tells us that ongoing, classroom-based assessment can serve this purpose. Teachers interacting with students will observe the nuances of their cognitive growth and development over time, their individual strengths and weaknesses in ways that would be extremely difficult, if not impossible, to capture through standardized or conventional testing alone (1995, p. 3).

There are two broad types of assessment teachers can use to support instruction. First is formative assessment that provides both immediate feedback to students and information to help a teacher keep instruction on track. Examples of formative assessments include practice tests and practice essays. Even a pop quiz, given a few days prior to the unit test, can serve as a formative assessment. Additional strategies for formative assessments include peer grading and self-reflection.

Formative assessments need to be carefully planned to address two goals. The first goal is to accurately assess student learning and so provide direction for instruction. A variety of traditional methods can be used, ranging from multiple-choice tests, written assignments, and projects, as well as nontraditional methods such as games and panel discussions. The traditional methods provide individual feedback and scores, while the nontraditional methods provide immediate feedback, but not individual scores. Another method is to have the students maintain journals that teachers periodically review to provide additional information on individual and class progress.

Test questions and activities for formative assessments should parallel those of the summative assessment. However, the two should not be identical. For example, a math teacher teaching students how to solve a time/distance problem could create several parallel problems. The formative assessment items should be similar, but different from those used on the unit assessment. The task is to teach the student how to solve the problem, not how to substitute one set of time-and-distance data for another.

The second goal of formative assessments is to provide meaningful feedback to the students. One approach is to discuss the items on a test. This discussion goes beyond simply giving the correct answer to providing information on why the answer is correct and why others are incorrect. Students should be involved in the discussion to encourage them to reflect on the information. A second approach is peer tutoring. Pair the students in the class and then have them grade and explain the correct answers. A third approach is to have students grade their own work, and then write explanations for the correct and incorrect responses.

Research evidence shows that high-quality, formative assessment can have a powerful impact on student learning. Black and Wiliam report that studies of formative assessment show an effect size on standardized tests of between 0.4 and 0.7, larger than most known educational interventions (1998).

In contrast to formative assessments, summative assessments are snapshots of a point in time of a student's learning. Examples include a test given as the unit test and a standardized test given once a year. The purpose of these tests is typically to measure student learning rather than to provide immediate feedback to the student or teacher.

Teachers might use these results to make changes for the next school year. They should also carefully consider the type of feedback they provide to students. Feedback on a summative assessment varies depending on the type of assessment. A standardized test often only provides a score as feedback. However, a teacher-developed assessment should provide the same opportunities for feedback to students as a formative assessment.

---

### The Potential Ripple Effect of Interim Assessments

Effective interim assessments can:

- Give teachers timely insights on the kinds of minute-by-minute classroom assessments that might nip student misconceptions and misunderstandings in the bud and prevent them from continuing week after week.
- Give teachers periodic feedback on whether their students are actually learning what's being taught—on what's working and what isn't working in the way they are orchestrating learning experiences.
- Give teachers feedback on ways to improve their unit and lesson planning for better student understanding and retention.
- Provide fine-grained data for teacher teams to analyze student learning results and plan improvements. These meetings are critical to improving teaching and learning and accelerating student achievement during the year.
- Identify students who need follow-up and the areas in which they need extra help; this could include skills and concepts that need to be retaught to the whole class, to small groups, or to individual students and information for tutors and after school programs.
- Contribute to far better results on summative assessments without resorting to the "junk food" of test prep.

In short, effective use of interim assessments helps principals see the *results* of what teachers do in classrooms rather than looking only at the *process* of instruction (Marshall, 2006a, p. 18).

---

## What Are You Looking For?

Thus far in this chapter we have hardly used the word data. But, obviously, generating data is the point of assessment. Data become the knowledge we need to improve instruction through the questions we ask when framing our analysis of the data—data from state assessments, data from end-of-unit tests, or even the type of data a teacher is constantly collecting when she watches students' faces for signs of understanding or confusion during a lesson.

At the teacher level, there are questions that should be asked continuously; for example,

- Are my teaching strategies working?
- What does this class need help with? What does this particular student need help with?
- What do students understand and what can they apply?
- What misconceptions do my students have? (North Carolina Department of Public Instruction, 1999).

> *"Challenging as it is, using data to improve teaching and learning is possible. In our experience, the key lies in building a school culture in which faculty members collaborate regularly and make instructional decisions based on evidence about students' skills and understanding"* (Boudett & Steele, 2007, p. 2).

## How Will You Look For It?

On a very basic level, teachers use data to identify ways to improve instruction. The first step is developing a plan—sometimes simply a mental framework—for organizing the data around important issues. One district has developed a structured process to help teachers focus on data questions and then to reflect on the answers as they strengthen their own use of instructional strategies (see Figure 4.1).

## Figure 4.1. Papillion-La Vista Schools: Applying Assessment Data to Instructional Improvement

**Classroom Goal: Background Information**

- What was the objective of the unit of study?
- What assessment method did you use?
- What strategies did you use to teach the objective?
- Based on the results of the assessment, what are the strengths of the students?
- Based on the results of the assessment, what are the weaknesses of the students?

**Classroom Goal: Action Plan**

SMART goals are specific, measurable, attainable, results-oriented, and time-bound. Example: My students will improve in writing in the traits of ideas and content as measured on the 6-trait scoring guide by the end of the first semester.

- My Classroom Goal (written as a SMART Goal).
- Instructional strategies or classroom activities I will use with my students.
- Describe the feedback you will give to students. *(For example: Will you provide specific and corrective feedback from a scoring guide? What will students do as a result of the feedback? Will students get feedback from other students?)*

**Classroom Goal: Action Plan Follow-up** (attach to original Classroom Goal Action Plan)

- Since the last Classroom Goals meeting, I implemented the following instructional strategies or classroom activities.
- Describe the feedback you gave to students. *(For example: Did you provide specific and corrective feedback from a scoring guide? What did students do as a result of the feedback? Did students get feedback from other students?)*
- Instructional strategies or classroom activities I will use before the next meeting

(Papillion-La Vista Schools, Nebraska. Information provided by Superintendent Jef Johnston).

Teacher use of data is supported by another element of this district's plan. Teachers are provided with time to talk about student work—again using a structured process. Teachers in all schools meet one day a month to evaluate results from a range of student assessments and to plan instruction based on the results. Principals create teams of 3 to 4 teachers, with each of the teams working together for the entire school year.

The classroom goals protocol developed by district staff developers and pilot teams of teachers is used to structure work of the teams:

> Prior to each month's meeting, each teacher prepares by selecting an area where students are struggling. The teacher collects student work, either a formative or common summative assessment that demonstrates where students are having difficulty. The teacher then uses the protocol's forms to prepare a brief analysis of students' performance and to outline the lesson focus and assessment task for background to share with the team. In addition to the completed form, teachers bring six samples of student work, representing two high-scoring students, two average-scoring students, and two low-scoring students. During the meeting, the team focuses on three questions:
>
> 1. Did your assessment match your instructional strategies?
> 2. What were student strengths?
> 3. What were student weaknesses? (Johnston, Knight, & Miller, 2007, p. 16).

During discussion, other teachers on the team suggest instructional strategies intended to address the area of concern. The teacher tries some of the suggested strategies, gathers data related to their impact, and returns to the group for more discussion the next month. The small size of the teams provides times for each of its members to discuss issues in depth.

In addition to these monthly "classroom goals" meetings, other teams in the elementary schools meet weekly to focus on: 1) curriculum planning and classroom assessment and 2) student interventions. Most elementary principals provide the time for these weekly 40-minute sessions by having teachers work together for 30 minutes before students arrive supplemented by 10-15 minutes during which other staff members—such as the literacy coach—lead short learning activities for students (Johnston, Knight, & Miller, 2007).

As the example above illustrates, schools and districts are finding that increasing the time and opportunities teachers have to review and discuss student work together can have positive impact on efforts to strengthen instruction. Another example of a way to structure teacher collaboration around analysis of student work—around data—is provided below.

## The Tuning Protocol

The Tuning Protocol, developed by the Coalition of Essential Schools, is a structured, facilitated conversation that involves a group of teachers (and sometimes others) in examining samples of student work to address a focusing question—usually about instructional practice or the quality of student work. It is often used as a way to address questions of goals or standards for an individual classroom or school.

A typical tuning protocol brings together a small group of teachers (10-15) with a facilitator who may come from outside or inside the school. One teacher (or a team of teachers) presents sample student work and the context for the work (the assignment or assessment rubric). The protocol follows a schedule calling for presentation of the task or project, clarifying questions, examination of student work samples, "warm" and "cool" feedback to presenting teacher(s), reflection by the presenting teacher, and debriefing of the process. The entire protocol takes about an hour and 15 minutes.

The protocol may be used as a "one-shot" instrument for addressing an important schoolwide question or issue or, probably more effectively, as part of ongoing professional development or planning. The Tuning Protocol can be modified and adjusted for use in the classroom as a peer review and exhibition tool.

### Guidelines for Looking at Student Work

The following guidelines were developed by the Philadelphia Education Fund to help teacher teams get started with a process of inquiry. These guidelines were informed by the work of a variety of education organizations and practitioners.

1.  Gather a team, or small group, of teachers together.
2.  Select a piece of student work. The sample should demonstrate a rich variety of student learning. It can be a work-in-progress, a final piece, or a document of a performance. Also collect the scoring guide or rubric used to assess that piece. Make copies for team members, if possible.
3.  If someone in the group is not familiar with your unit of study, take a few minutes to introduce its overall purpose, the activities that have been conducted, and the work that has been generated.
4.  Discuss and write down one standard from…(those) that you expected students to address in this activity. What did you expect the students to know and be able to do?
5.  Next, take a few minutes to look at the work as a group. Either read it aloud, or let each person take a turn looking at it.
6.  Write down the group's observations about the work. Then write down comments and questions. You might allow each team member to do this first individually and then share in turn.
7.  Next, use your scoring guide or rubric to assess the piece of work. If you do not yet have a scoring guide, re-read the standard you have identified and assess the work based on its criteria. (You might put together an informal rubric by doing this.)
8.  Take a few minutes to discuss as a team the following questions: What can you see from your observations, comments, and questions that will help you assess student learning? How might these observations determine your next steps as a teacher? Do these observations tell you anything new about your unit of study or classroom activities?

(Philadelphia Education Fund, n.d.).

## How Will You Use the Data?

Data from assessments, whether formative or summative, should be examined from a variety of perspectives. Teachers should be looking for indicators—for patterns—in the data so that they can make the necessary classroom or learning accommodations for the class as a whole or for individual students.

This is another stage at which we need to ask questions to help discover meaning in the data. And again, it is important to ask the "right" questions. Asking *which* students are *not* meeting standards in reading as well as *how many* students are meeting standards provide two different data points, both of which may be important to identifying needed adjustments to instruction. Examples of useful questions may be:

- How often did the students demonstrate…?
- How did different children (or teams) differ on…?
- Which students/teams did…? How well?
- Where are the gaps? What was disappointing?
- What worked?
- What different approaches can I use to address a learning gap?
- Where do I/we need to change and improve?
- What strategies are most apt to create?
- Which strategies need to be abandoned as ineffective?

The next step is an action step that takes answers to questions such as these and puts into place changes—sometimes little tweaks, sometimes large shifts—intended to improve instruction for an entire class or, sometimes, for one child. Some of these changes may happen in the classroom. Other times, a student may need additional supports outside the scope of his or her regular classroom.

## Your Role as Principal

Meyers and Rust stress the importance of helping teachers learn how to "assess their own work and its impact on their students" (2000, p. 34). To be successful, school leaders need to engage in conversations with teachers, using assessment data to diagnose strengths as well as areas in which the teachers need to modify their instruction. In addition, by providing teachers with time and opportunity for discussion that uses assessment data as a springboard, principals can strengthen a school's instructional program.

# Notes, Reminders, and Ideas:

_____

_____

_____

_____

_____

_____

_____

_____

_____

_____

_____

_____

_____

_____

_____

_____

_____

_____

_____

_____

_____

_____

_____

_____

_____

_____

# Notes, Reminders, and Ideas:

# Chapter 5
# Using Data to Catch and Address Reading Problems Early

*What are you looking for?*
*How will you look for it?*
*How will you use the data?*

*"Frequent assessment of developing readers, and the use of that information for planning instruction, is the most reliable way of preventing children from falling behind and staying behind"* (Learning First Alliance, 2000, p. 23).

Although we have already talked about ways in which teachers can use assessment data to strengthen instructional planning, one specific area—reading instruction—deserves special attention. Children in the primary grades are expected to develop a wide variety of reading-related skills rapidly. In many classes, differences in experiences outside school, as well as other readiness and cognitive factors, translate into a wide range of skills. If teachers do not have timely assessment data available to them, instruction for many of these children can be off target.

Many states now require standardized early literacy assessments, with the results available on a school-by-school or even a classroom-by-classroom basis. This information is particularly helpful when the results include detailed analyses about the mastery of individual skills. Used as a diagnostic tool, such data can help guide instruction at the school, classroom, and student levels (Denton, 1999).

Additional classroom-based assessments of children, many of them informal and embedded in instruction, also let the classroom teacher know whether all children in the class are progressing toward key objectives or whether some children need instruction in specific areas. A report issued by the Connecticut Department of Education talks about some ways teachers can use assessment data in planning reading instruction:

> Assessment can assist the teacher in planning flexible groups and in determining which children need more instruction—or, conversely, a greater level of challenge—in a particular competency or set of competencies. Because individual children will acquire various competencies at different rates, ongoing assessment is necessary for re-evaluating children's needs and reconstituting flexible groups on a regular basis (2000, p. 59).

## A Focus on Children Experiencing Difficulty

In recent years, research has stressed the need to apply assessment data to identification of students with reading-related difficulties and provision of additional help before they fall too far behind. Research has shown that assessment in kindergarten can be key to catching problems early, because:

> 85% of those children likely to become poor readers can be identified with tests of their abilities to manipulate letter sounds, to rapidly name letters and numbers, and to demonstrate an awareness of the concepts of print (Special Education Division, California Department of Education, 2000, p. 6).

Intervention that takes place early on—in kindergarten through second grade or even during the preschool years—can help get children off to a good start in reading and prevent the need for remediation in the upper grades. For an estimated 90 - 95% of these children, prevention and early intervention programs that include good instruction in phonemic awareness, phonics, reading comprehension strategies and fluency development can increase reading skills to average levels (Lyon, 1998). However, "if we delay early intervention until 9 years of age (the time that most children with reading difficulties first receive services), approximately 75% of these children will continue to have difficulties learning to read throughout their high school and adult years" (Lyon, 1997).

## What Are You Looking For?

Although this "what are you looking for?" question is primarily directed at your teachers, your leadership is important for the direction it provides to other school staff.

In an effort to identify practices and interventions that promote positive literacy outcomes for preschool children, the National Early Literacy Panel (NELP) conducted a synthesis of research on early literacy development of young children. Through their review of 300 peer-reviewed studies, the panel identified the skills and abilities of preschool and kindergarten children that are predictors of future reading achievement. Their findings emphasized the importance of several early literacy components, specifically:

- alphabet knowledge, including such things as rapid naming tasks involving either naming of letters and digits or naming of objects and colors,
- phonological awareness,
- writing/writing name, and
- phonological short-term memory (2007, p. 1).

Students who lack age-appropriate levels of these skills are less likely to keep up with their classmates as reading instruction moves forward to increasingly more complex skills. Thus, assessments should provide the data needed to diagnose possible difficulties in each of these areas.

Other sources of "what students should be able to do" at particular grade levels are your state and district standards. Many of these standards provide common-sense indicators of what to look for to gauge whether a student is on track. Other indicators are also available. For example, the Northwest Regional Educational Laboratory has developed the *K-3 Developmental Continuum*, a rubrics-based system that assigns reading related skills to the five stages of reading competence. Teachers can use this guide to assess student strengths and weaknesses and to set performance goals. See Figure 5.1 for a rubric for "establishing comprehension."

## Figure 5.1. Rubric for "Establishing Comprehension" for Five Stages of Reading Competence

Emerging

- Making meaningful predictions based on illustrations.
- Identifying characters in a story.
- Relying on illustrations more heavily than print for meaning.

Beginning

- Using sentence strategies with modeling and guidance.
- Finding the "main character" in a story.
- Retelling beginning, middle, and end with guidance.
- Relying on illustrations and print.

Developing

- Using pre-reading strategies during reading, and post-reading strategies with deliberation.
- Distinguishing between an obvious major and minor character.
- Retelling beginning, middle, and end by self.
- Summarizing with references to single "parts" of stories—characters, plot, and setting.
- Using reading strategies consistently.

Expanding

- Learning that a "detail" is used to describe an element of a story.
- Summarizing "whole" stories in addition to their parts.
- Summarizing a literary "purpose" (explaining the moral of fable, for example) with guidance.
- Relying primarily on print to establish understanding.

Bridging

- Actively seeking print to gain understanding (I want to read to find out).
- Beginning to distinguish between significant and supporting detail.
- Summarizing whole stories and parts of stories with ease.

Source: Northwest Regional Education Laboratory (2000)

**Ask these questions to evaluate your school's early literacy assessment procedures:**

- Is the assessment procedure based on the goals and objectives of the specific curriculum used in the program?
- Are the results of assessment used to benefit children, i.e., to plan for individual children, improve instruction, identify children's interests and needs, and individualize instruction, rather than label, track, or fail children?
- Does assessment provide useful information to teachers to help them do a better job?
- Is the teacher the primary assessor and are teachers adequately trained for this role?
- Are the screening tests used reliable and valid for the purpose for which they are used? Are the technical adequacies of standardized measures carefully evaluated by knowledgeable professionals?
- Is there a systematic procedure for collecting assessment data that facilitates its use in planning instruction and communicating with parents.

(National Association for the Education of Young Children and National Association of Early Childhood Specialists in State Departments of Education, 1990, p. 34-35)

## How Will You Look For It?

There is no prescribed formula for early literacy assessment. Rather, a mixture of formal and informal methods should be used, based on the abilities and needs of students as well as the specific purposes for which the data will be used. Because students' literacy skills change over time and must be evaluated frequently, assessment measures should be easy to administer, easily repeated, and both time and cost efficient (Kame'enui & Simmons, 1998).

To be effective, assessment should be an ongoing process that provides data to inform and improve literacy instruction for both individual students and whole-group instruction (Tierney 1998). While the use of standardized tests is increasingly common, no single assessment tool can provide a complete picture of a child's literacy progress or achievement. Additionally, no single test can meet the needs of all groups who require information about school and student performance. Multiple forms of assessment, many of which can occur as part of instructional situations, help to illuminate patterns of a child's literacy learning behavior. These assessments include informal assessments, formal assessments, and authentic assessments. When combined as a comprehensive snapshot of a student's literacy growth, these multiple assessments provide valuable information for teachers as they work to meet the learning needs of individual students.

## Formal Assessments

The term "formal assessment" often brings to mind visions of children sitting in straight rows filling in "bubbles" on a standardized achievement test. While this vision may not be entirely applicable to early grades reading assessment, the reality is that some young students do participate in assessments administered under standardized conditions to measure their literacy achievement (Walker, 2008). In some instances, depending on the grade level, these tests include multiple-choice items designed to measure a specific reading skill. For younger students, such tests may be administered orally, with students prompted to circle or point to a word represented by a picture.

A number of formal early literacy assessments are currently in use, including:

- **Dynamic Indicators of Basic Early Literacy Skills (DIBELS®)**:  DIBELS assessments are individualized and standardized measures of early literacy development. Using short, one-minute fluency measures, teachers use DIBELS measurements to monitor the development of their students' early reading skills. These measures assess a reader's knowledge of initial sounds, letter naming, phoneme segmentation, nonsense words, oral reading, retelling, and word use. Teachers can use the results of the assessment to measure individual student progress and determine how an individual student compares with peers. However-er, researchers Schilling, Carlisle, Scott, and Zeng (2007) caution that DIBELS should be used in conjunction with other assessments because DIBELS may understate problems some children are having with comprehension. In one New Mexico district, teachers of the early grades use this comprehensive approach. DIBELS testing three times a year is supplemented with frequent one-minute assessments to monitor progress. Teachers use the data to adjust instruction for children in their classes. In addition, grade level teams meet at least monthly to discuss data from these assessments (Olson, 2007). (NOTE: DIBELS assessments are available online at no charge, although there is a charge for use of the online recording system. Go to http://dibels.uoregon.edu)

- **Individual Growth and Development Indicators (IGDI)**: Like DIBELS, IGDI assessments are used to monitor important developmental domains, such as language, social, cognitive, and motor development. While DIBELS is intended to be used with children in kindergarten and beyond, IGDIs are designed to be used with preschoolers who are 3 to 5 years old. IGDIs that assess early reading development include tasks such as letter naming, alliteration, rhyming, and picture naming. IGDIs can be used repeatedly over short periods of time. These assessment tools can help to identify children's learning needs and can evaluate the effectiveness of instructional interventions (Early Childhood Research Institute on Measuring Growth and Development, 1998).

- **Phonological Awareness Literacy Screening (PALS)**: PALS-PreK is a formal assessment tool that evaluates name writing, alphabet knowledge, beginning sound awareness, print and word awareness, rhyme awareness, and nursery rhyme awareness. At the kindergarten level, the screening assesses a child's knowledge of the alphabetic code, phonological awareness (specifically rhyme and beginning sound), and ability to recognize lower-case letters. These scientifically based screenings measure the skills that predict future literacy success. Teachers administer this assessment at the beginning of the year and use the results to help guide instruction. When students are assessed again at the end of the year, the results of the test are used to evaluate student progress. This program, originally developed for use by Virginia teachers, now has screenings available for additional grades and an online system into which teachers enter results. PALS data can be used by teachers as they assign students to reading groups or identify students who need supplemental help.

*"Observations, anecdotes, and daily work samples are certainly low-stakes evidence of achievement for accountability purposes, but they may be the most useful for teachers"* (Paris & Hoffman, 2004, p. 205).

## Informal Assessments

Although formal assessment measures such as the PALS program, as well as "traditional" standardized tests, provide useful data for instructional decision making, the value of more informal assessment measures is becoming widely recognized. Informal assessments are conducted to understand what students do as they engage in the process of reading and writing. For inexperienced readers who do not yet read and write conventionally, process-oriented assessments include observations of what they do as they attempt to read and write. During reading, the teacher may note how the child is holding a book, "reading" the illustrations, or noticing print. During writing, the teacher may observe the interactions that occur as children write with others and ask children about the meaning of their work.

For students who have made the transition into reading, two informal assessments can be essential to understanding their reading process: *running records* and *miscue analysis*. Running records are diagnostic notes the teacher makes as a child reads aloud a passage from a text. Using a series of checkmarks for words read correctly, and notations for words incorrectly omitted, inserted, or misread, the running record provides a wealth of information to the teacher about the student as a reader. Running records help teachers note a child's reading fluency—phrasing, smoothness, and pace when reading a text (Opitz & Rasinski, 1991). The observation also provides the teacher with information about the child's reading habits and comfort level with the text.

After collecting a running record of the students' reading process, teachers can analyze the errors the reader made. This process, called miscue analysis, helps teachers understand the ways their students read texts (Goodman, 1973). Teachers analyze the errors by determining whether the reader is using semantic, syntactic, or phonographic cues to read unfamiliar words. Throughout the school year, multiple running records with miscue analysis provide a clear picture of what children do as they are engaged in reading.

Informal Reading Inventories (IRIs) are informal assessments teachers administer to understand student progress in reading and writing. They are often administrated three times during an academic school year—at the beginning of the school year to obtain baseline data, during the middle of the year to chart progress, and at the end of the year to note literacy growth. During these assessments, students read passages orally and silently and answer comprehension questions about the passage. When students read orally, the teacher takes running records and notes the readers' fluency. The teacher then evaluates the student as a reader to match the student with texts that he or she can read independently or with instructional assistance.

Teachers, especially, can see first-hand the benefits of informal assessments. For instance, techniques such as running records, anecdotal records, informal reading inventories, and observation provide teachers with immediate feedback that can be used to improve and adjust the instructional methods used with individual children. In addition, these assessments can be embedded in regular classroom instruction. Teachers should be encouraged to look at the activities they conduct every day and to ask themselves, "What does this tell me about the students in my class?"

Consider this example: a fourth-grade teacher conducts an "assessment interview" while meeting with a small group of students during reading workshop. She hands each student a copy of the book being used and asks them to look at the cover, title, and illustrations. As the students do this, they discuss what they notice, generate questions, and predict what the book may be about. After this initial activity, students read the book individually, stopping to discuss their thoughts, reactions, and questions as necessary. Although the teacher has a few prompts for discussion, she mainly allows conversational topics to be determined by the students.

As the students discuss the story, the teacher can glean information about each child's comprehension of the story, the reading strategies each child is using, and each child's level of engagement with the text. She is also able to observe reading behavior—use of word attack strategies and rereading, amount of fidgeting, and reading speed—as she watches them read independently (Harvey & Goudvis, 2000). A technique such as an assessment interview can easily be embedded in classroom instruction and provides teachers with a wealth of information about a child's reading skills.

---

### Story Construction from a Picture Book: An Informal Assessment Activity for Young Learners

Christina E. Van Kraayenoord and Scott G. Paris developed an assessment activity called "Story Construction from a Picture Book" as a performance-based, "authentic" assessment of young children's skills in comprehending and describing the relationship among a series of pictures. The activity provides information about young children's meaning making even if children do not yet have clear concepts about print or if they are just beginning to develop literacy behaviors.

To conduct the assessment, choose a picture book with an identifiable narrative. Then, ask a child to tell you the "story" by reading the pictures. The story line that the child develops reveals much about the child's understanding of the information, actions, and feelings in the story and the child's emerging skill at expanding the story beyond the information given. Because the activity does not use printed text, the authors suggest that it may be particularly useful for those students whose first language is not English.

(Excerpted from Van Kraayenoord & Paris, 1996).

---

## Authentic Assessment

Teachers are also finding that "authentic" activities—for example, asking even primary students to write a letter—can be embedded in classroom instruction and provide immediate feedback concerning students' strengths and weaknesses. For example, does a second-grader demonstrate that he understands the meaning of punctuation marks by using them appropriately?  Examples of authentic activities include:

- anecdotal observations made by the teacher while a child engages in reading or writing,
- samples of student work, such as writing samples and artwork, that are maintained in portfolios,

- audiotapes of students reading aloud or engaged in discussions about books that have been read aloud to them,
- surveys and interviews that reveal students' attitudes and interests,
- conferences in which the teacher meets one-on-one with an individual child to assess a particular literacy skill, and
- checklists that are comprised of a list of developmental behaviors or skills (Morrow, 2005).

> *"Early reading instruction, coupled with intervention for at-risk children, can prevent many children from ever getting caught in the downward spiral of school failure"* (Wilson & Protheroe, 2002, p. 101).

## How Will You Use the Data?

Wilson and Protheroe discuss the issue of early intervention for children experiencing difficulties learning to read:

> Both research and practice are helping to identify ways to identify and help students who are judged likely to have difficulty before the barrier becomes insurmountable.

> Preventive interventions are most efficient if they target the children with the greatest need for special instruction, a goal that can be achieved if accurate identification procedures are in place. Every effort should be made to ensure that children's reading problems are recognized and addressed early, before the "critical period" for learning to read passes and reading problems begin to interfere with the acquisition of content knowledge (2002, p. 53).

Consider the following criteria when reviewing your current program (again, using data from a variety of sources such as both formal and informal assessments as well as classroom observations):

- It must be "intensive enough to close the ever-widening gap between poor readers and their grade level peers as quickly as possible."
- It should be grounded in research about the acquisition of reading skills.
- The intervention must "match the student's level of reading because each stage of growth requires a special focus."
- For very poor readers, the instruction must be designed to develop students' phonological skills since their inability to correctly identify speech sounds typically acts as a barrier to developing other reading related skills.
- Text reading fluency should be the target for instruction for less impaired readers who *can* decipher words through sounds. Vocabulary development should be targeted through direct instruction as well as through providing opportunities for and encouraging extensive reading (Moats, 2001, p, 37).

Steinberg (1998) suggests that instruction for struggling readers should also include more time for reading and writing than that scheduled for students who are not having problems. He recommends that special instruction—tutoring, small-group instruction, etc.—be provided on a daily basis for most, if not the entire school year. As principal, you can encourage and provide administrative support for such regrouping of children who are struggling with reading. Assessment data can be used to help establish groups of children that receive different types of instruction based on their competencies and weaknesses. To support more skills-based and individualized instruction, you might establish a common time for reading instruction across the school. Some schools support this approach by assigning all instructional staff as reading teachers during this time period. Thus, some groups—those with students needing intensive help—can have very low pupil-teacher ratios.

## What Are the Principal's Responsibilities?

Obviously, most of the day-to-day work involved in assessing children's reading-related skills falls to teachers; however, principals can play an important role in ensuring teachers understand the importance of collecting, interpreting, and then using reading assessment data to plan and deliver instruction designed to ensure the needs of individual children—especially those who are struggling—are met. An effective reading program overall provides the best foundation for meeting these needs.

First, use results from assessments to determine the strengths and weaknesses of your school's reading program. For example, the results may indicate that second-grade students in your school scored well on word recognition skills, but poorly on reading comprehension. Does this information point to a problem with the emphasis placed on the two areas in your reading program's scope and sequence? Or do teachers need additional development in ways to strengthen comprehension instruction? Schools that have effectively evaluated and restructured their reading programs begin by studying the goals they have for student learning. They analyze assessment data to identify problem areas and then ask: "How can we better prepare our teachers to address both our goals and problems that have been identified?"

Second, you can provide opportunities for development and conversation around the critical area of developing and using assessments. Teachers might need help in: 1) how to better design and analyze results from assessments of the type they have always conducted; and 2) how to quickly and efficiently conduct periodic assessments of individual students. As a second step, grade level teachers—and even cross-grade teams—might meet together to discuss assessment results, often selecting a few children as the focus. Questions addressed might include instructional strategies to better meet the needs of these children or ways to regroup them for skills-based instruction.

Third, you can review approaches your school uses to support struggling students. Since school resources, staff time, and student time are limited, it is vital to implement programs that are most likely to be effective in providing extra help to below-grade-level readers.

Finally, support efforts to identify approaches to assessment that might yield useful data—while keeping teacher time needed to administer, record, and analyze assessments to a minimum. For example, some schools use handheld devices to record results from DIBELS assessment. The data are then transferred to a computer—with the analysis available on a web-based system.

# Notes, Reminders, and Ideas:

_____

_____

_____

_____

_____

_____

_____

_____

_____

_____

_____

_____

_____

_____

_____

_____

_____

_____

_____

_____

_____

_____

_____

_____

_____

_____

_____

_____

# Chapter 6

# Using Data to Assess the Effectiveness of School Programs

*What are you looking for?*
*How will you look for it?*
*How will you use the data?*

*"Evaluation, at its core, is simple and useful: Finding what works and what doesn't"* (Kaufman, Guerra, & Platt, 2006, p. 1).

Another important use of data in schools is in evaluation of programs. The word *program* here is used broadly. It could apply to something as large as an after-school tutoring program, perhaps a particular approach to teaching reading, or maybe something even more defined such as the use of a specific instructional strategy. The important point is that schools—and, especially, you as the school's leader—should be constantly looking at what school personnel are doing and then asking: "Is what we are doing having a positive impact on students?"

Program evaluation can help to answer a range of common-sense—but critically important—questions. For example, "Are things going as planned?" "Are we beginning to see the results we anticipated?" "What changes should we make, if any, to ensure success?" (Mid-continent Research for Education and Learning, 2000). Cicchinelli and Barley (1999) suggest that evaluations can also focus on another essential element of program effectiveness and ask the question, "Did you do what you intended to?" This is a particularly important question in schools since a program or approach that has previously been effective in other settings can be ineffective in yours if the way it is being implemented takes it far away from the program's intended design. Guskey adds some additional perspectives on questions an evaluation can address:

> We use evaluations to determine the value of something—to help answer such questions as, Is this program or activity achieving its intended results? Is it better than what was done in the past? Is it better than another, competing activity? Is it worth the costs? (Guskey, 2002, p. 46).

Finally, Howard steps back from the idea of evaluating one specific program and puts the approach in a broader context:

> School improvement and data-driven decision making are two terms that all school leaders hear almost every day. Program evaluation brings together these two concepts by focusing data collection and analysis in an organized way in order to improve programs and, through improvement of these component programs, to improve schools (2004, p. 1).

---

*"Quite simply, evaluation means taking a closer look at and getting feedback about an undertaking, with an eye to making a decision about its value. In schools, program evaluation means examining initiatives the school has undertaken—whether the initiative is an approach to literacy instruction or a program to support struggling students—to answer the question, 'Is what we are doing working?'"* (Center for Comprehensive School Reform and Improvement, 2006, p. 2).

## Just What IS This Thing Called Evaluation, Anyway?

Consider this interchange:

"How did you like that restaurant we went to?"

"I thought it was good. The fish was very fresh, caught today. The servings were huge! And the menu was great—over 20 selections. How about you? What did you think?"

"Well, it didn't impress me much. The waiter took over 10 minutes just to bring us water. And they were all out of the blueberry pie!"

"Hmm, I gave it high marks and you flunked it. I guess we need to go back again to get some more data!"

We have just witnessed an evaluation taking place. It happens all the time. Which fruit to buy? Which shirt to wear? What TV program to watch? You are an evaluator. We are all evaluators. Evaluation is so much a part of everyday life that we often don't even notice when we are doing it. It is a necessary part of our lives and a skill that we need to survive, as well as to better our lives. If the fish in the restaurant had not been cooked properly and we incorrectly evaluated it as fresh, that would definitely be a threat to our health.

Evaluation is simply judging the value of something.

Program evaluation is simply making this same kind of judgment about a program. Is it being carried out correctly (did the water arrive on time)? Is it having the kinds of effects it set out to accomplish (were the servings adequate)? What were the activities (the menu)? What were the outcomes (how did the meal taste)?

How do we make these kinds of judgments? We gather evidence. Some things are easier to gather evidence about than others. How long the waiter took to bring us water can be measured with a wristwatch. And either they had blueberry pie or they did not. Yes or no. When it is something like this, that can be measured by anyone and the answer would be the same, we call it "objective" evidence. Some things are more difficult to measure. How fresh was the fish? How do we know? By the color? By the texture? Maybe by the waiter telling us it was caught today! When the available evidence is that of our senses we call it "subjective."

When we are evaluating educational programs, usually the more objective the evidence, the better. Evaluating a textbook or a new teaching technique, for example, can involve some pretty heavy consequences. We don't want our kids "eating a poisonous fish"; we want their educational meal to be adequate and nutritious! (Hammond, 2006, p. 11).

## But We Can't Do a Program Evaluation!

While you might agree in theory with the idea that data should be collected to assess how well programs are working, you might also be thinking, "We don't have the time or skills needed for this evaluation 'thing'?" You are definitely not alone in that opinion.

> Many believe that evaluation is a highly unique and complex process that occurs at a certain time in a certain way, and almost always includes the use of outside experts. Many people believe they must completely understand terms such as validity and reliability. They don't have to. They do have to consider what information they need in order to make current decisions about program issues or needs. And they have to be willing to commit to understanding what is really going on…. [Otherwise,] they miss precious opportunities to make more of a difference for their customer and clients, or to get a bigger bang for their buck (McNamara, 1998).

Herman and Winters suggest that educators long-term experience as "progress trackers" who gather a range of data intended to help assess what is going on in classrooms prepares them well for program evaluation. They continue, "Much of this progress tracking, whether at the classroom or program level, addresses two simple questions: How are we doing? How can we improve?" (1992, p. 7).

McNamara agrees that educators have the skills and ability to conduct evaluations, since they:

> do not have to be experts in these topics to carry out a useful program evaluation. The '20-80' rule applies here, that 20% of effort generates 80% of the needed results. It's better to do what might turn out to be an average effort at evaluation than to do no evaluation at all (McNamara, 1998).

In addition, "many evaluation techniques are easy to execute; can make use of data that are already being gathered; and can be performed on a scale that is practical for teachers, principals, and other school leaders" (Center for Comprehensive School Reform and Improvement, 2006, p. 1-2).

> *"Good evaluations don't have to be complicated. They simply require thoughtful planning, the ability to ask good questions, and a basic understanding of how to find valid answers"* (Guskey, 2002, p. 46).

Most schools don't have the resources to hire an outside person to help with a program evaluation—but are also concerned about the staff time it will take. Howard addresses the resource issue. In her view, an evaluation can be organized to make efficient use of staff time. In addition, developing the skills for program evaluation among school staff produces an additional benefit: it helps to build a school culture of reflective practice and continuous improvement.

The challenge, then, is to conduct an evaluation so it yields useful data—while not diverting undue amounts of staff time from teaching and other important responsibilities. We again will use our three questions—What are you looking for? How will you look for it? How will you use the data?—to help structure the process.

## What Are You Looking For?

Obviously, you will have some very specific questions you are attempting to answer. However, it might be helpful to look at some broad purposes of program evaluation and use these to help define your questions—in essence, the purpose of your evaluation. Howard talks about these purposes—a program evaluation can focus on any or all of the following:

- **Assessing program efficacy.** Is the program or activity demonstrating effectiveness? Is the program meeting its stated goals and objectives? Of course, it is most useful to focus on such questions when the program has clearly defined goals and objectives.

- **Taking stock.** How well is the program being implemented? Are there variations across classrooms? Do particular components seem to be strengthening the overall program? How has the addition of technology affected the reading program's effectiveness? Have students using a newly introduced software program, intended to strengthen phonemic awareness, demonstrated higher achievement in reading? Has student motivation increased with the use of a particular software program?

- **Problem solving.** If the program seems to have problems, what is the nature of the problems and what are some possible solutions? For example, if you already know from discussions with teachers that some teachers are highly satisfied with the reading program, while others have less positive opinions, a well-designed program evaluation might help to identify the source of these differing opinions. Perhaps the more positive teachers received better training in use of the program. Or perhaps the program is more successful with some students than with others, and the dissatisfied teachers are concerned about the students who are falling behind (2004, p. 6).

Howard also talks about the importance of carefully defining the purpose of the evaluation:

An ill-defined purpose can result in ambiguous or off-target findings that do not enhance decision making. A question that is too narrowly defined may lead to results that are meaningless at a programmatic level. Conversely, a question that is too broadly defined may lead to contradictory or even incoherent results (2004, p. 18).

---

### Program Evaluation for Decision Making: Links in a Chain

A critical component of planning is defining the purpose of the evaluation. A clear purpose will make it easier to develop and clarify the research questions so that you can gather appropriate evidence to support the eventual decision making that will follow the evaluation. You may find it helpful to think of each of these steps as a link in a chain. As each link is strengthened, the chain itself becomes stronger. The stronger the chain, the more useful the overall evaluation becomes as a tool for program improvement.

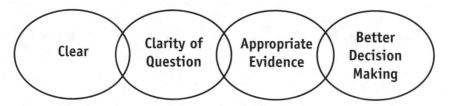

Source: Howard 2004, p. 17-18

## Formative Evaluations

Although many formal program evaluations may be summative in nature—asking whether a program had met its goals—formative evaluations are likely to be most helpful to your school's improvement efforts. There is a common sense reason for this. Periodic reviews of how things are going can help you ensure that programs, use of specific teaching strategies, etc., are headed in the right direction. Formative evaluations can help:

- determine whether the program is being implemented as the program developers designed it and that the most vital components of the program are in place, and
- enable staff to retool and fine-tune their efforts to make a program work at a specific site. A strong formative evaluation can help a program to "hum" at a particular school (Yap, Aldersebaes, Railsback, Shaughnessy, & Speth, 2000, p. 19).

Both of these elements are particularly important to a school staff's efforts to implement a program new to the school or a particular group of teachers.

## Developing Key Questions

Certainly, you will have a purpose for the evaluation—one that may be broad or fairly narrowly focused. But it is the question creation step that really defines the evaluation. The importance of spending time and careful thought developing these cannot be overstated, since "ultimately, the way the questions are worded will affect the kinds of conclusions that can be drawn about the program" (Yap, Aldersebaes, Railsback, Shaughnessy, & Speth, 2000, p. 24). They will also affect the kinds of data that will be needed and how it will need to be analyzed. Questions should be: clear, specific, pertinent to essential aspects or components of implementation of the program, and focused on a manageable set of issues (Yap et al., 2000, p.24).

## How Will You Look For It?

The "how" should begin with developing a thorough plan of action. Just as we know that teachers are more effective when they develop comprehensive lesson plans, an evaluation will be more effective and easier to conduct when you spend time on careful and detailed planning. As part of the planning process, you will need to:

- Establish due dates and timelines. Be realistic when assigning the amount of time needed—both staff hours and calendar time—for specific aspects of the evaluation. Planning too tightly almost guarantees that there will be slippage, and the overall project may suffer.
- Identify resources to aid in the evaluation. Although you may already have had some discussions about the resources available for the project, it is important at this stage to begin to align those resources with elements of the evaluation. Staff time and expertise are two resources that should be discussed in detail.
- Identify the components of the evaluation and assign responsibilities. Obviously the components of every program evaluation will be unique. The important thing at this stage is to think concretely—and in as detailed a manner as possible—about what will need to be done. As principal, you have had experience with managing many complex tasks. The evaluation team will need your expertise during this phase. If the team talks only in generalities about what will need to be done and fails to focus on the details, stop the discussion and use some examples to demonstrate the level of planning that will be needed.

One important piece of advice: Keep the plan as simple as possible, especially for your first evaluation. Remember that everyone working on the evaluation has other responsibilities, and that the evaluation will need to mesh with the normal flow of school work.

## Data Needed for the Evaluation

Once the key questions have been identified, the staff members working on the evaluation can focus on deciding what information (data) will be needed to answer them. In Champion's view,

> There are no Swiss army knives when it comes to data. No single data source can measure everything…. A good evaluation includes several kinds of data that measure the same thing from different angles (2002).

But, trying to draw from too many data sources may prove confusing. The goal is to develop an evaluation plan that balances the need for information with ease and cost of data collection. To do this, you must decide what information is critical to answering the question. You may also find that some of the relevant data may be difficult or expensive (in terms of time and money) to collect. Circle back to your questions and ask whether different ones—ones that could be addressed more economically—would still provide you with a productive evaluation.

When considering evidence for an evaluation, most people think of information that can be counted or measured numerically—student grades, standardized test scores, attendance records, and so on. It can be very useful because it is often easy to obtain and can be analyzed using statistical techniques. However, descriptions of how the program functions or the feelings and attitudes of those involved with the program also may be useful data to collect. Data of this sort can provide context and help to explain what the program means to those involved with it. Qualitative information may include surveys, interviews, or observations.

> *"One of the fundamental principles of program evaluation is that the evaluation should not be done if it is not going to be used"* (Sanders & Sullins, 2006, p. 59).

One school scheduled weekly staff development breakout sessions focused on introducing teachers to new instructional strategies or discussing ones they were already using. Short evaluations were used as a way to keep the quality of these programs high and the content relevant to teachers' needs.

Wednesday Morning Breakout Session Evaluation

Date: _____

Session: _____

The topic was timely and applicable.            ❏ Yes      ❏ No

The information presented was useful.            ❏ Yes      ❏ No

I would like another session on this topic.      ❏ Yes      ❏ No

I would recommend this session to a colleague.   ❏ Yes      ❏ No

The best part of the session was:

_____

_____

Something I would change about the session is:

_____

_____

(Standerfer, 2005, p.18)

## How Will You Use the Data?

Using the data is essential; otherwise, the resources used to support it would have been better spent elsewhere. Using the data has two components—analyzing it in order to glean "lessons" from it and then using these lessons to support decision making about next steps. Killion talks about the first component:

Interpretation is the "meaning-making" process that comes after the data have been counted, sorted, analyzed, and displayed" (2002, p. 109).

McNamara suggests that this meaning-making is often easier if you go back to the goals of your evaluation—the questions you wanted to answer:

This will help you organize your data and focus your analysis. For example, if you wanted to improve your program by identifying its strengths and weaknesses, you can organize data into program strengths, weaknesses, and suggestions to improve the program (1998).

Here are some additional "tips" that can help you and the other staff members analyzing the data that has been collected:

- Ask: "Do these results make sense? How can they help in decision making about the program?"
- Look at your data from a variety of perspectives. Talking about the information in team meetings may result in a broader and deeper understanding of its meaning than solitary analysis.
- Don't rush this step of the evaluation process. The first "fact" discovered may not be the most important one.
- Don't assume the program is the only source of outcomes (both positive and negative).
- Don't make too much of small differences between groups. A factor such as nonresponse bias may be contributing to this difference.
- Don't over-generalize the findings. They should reflect only the data gathered and analyzed in the evaluation (Cicchinelli & Barley, 1999; W.K. Kellogg Foundation, 1998).

## Applying Data to Decision Making

One of the uses of program evaluation data is to inform decision making about school programs. In schools that engage in a cycle of continuous improvement, the analysis of evidence—not opinions or unsupported beliefs—drives decision making (Jandris,

2001). Depending on the purpose of the evaluation, the team will need to consider the following.

- Does the program do what it is supposed to do?
- What program improvements do the findings suggest? If you decide to keep the current program, perhaps with modifications, the findings may suggest some program improvements.
- If the evaluation provides solid data that a program isn't working—and likely will not work, what does the evaluation tell us about what to look for in a new program?

The Arlington Virginia Public Schools' overview of its evaluation process includes some key points that should be part of the discussion of data analysis and the reporting of data. The key points include: the ways in which the programs or services should be improved, revised, continued or discontinued, by addressing the relative effectiveness of the approach; the worth or merit of that which was evaluated; recommendations regarding continuity and revisions; and recommendations for next steps (1999, p. 3-4).

---

**Common Challenges to Evaluation**

- Lack of time and resources
- Lack of training in "practical" program evaluation
- Fear of evaluation (Yap, Aldersebaes, Railsback, Shaughnessy, & Speth, 2000, p. 18).

---

## What Not To Do

The process we have been discussing requires careful planning, attention to detail, and your leadership to ensure it is done well. We have focused on the to-do's of good practice; however, looking at factors that can result in an ineffective evaluation can also help in your planning efforts. McNeely (2006) lists what she describes as "common evaluation mistakes." The evaluation:

- is conducted primarily as a "final product" with no follow up action,
- doesn't fit the specific school improvement goals of the projects,
- doesn't assign strong focus to student achievement outcomes,
- doesn't give strong focus to schools' (teachers') ability to implement the program,
- report is not written in a format to inform practice, or
- forgets that its purpose is to be a critical friend.

Finally, Kaufman, Guerra, and Platt stress that "evaluation data must be used for improving and never blaming" (2006, p. 2).

## Other Ways Principals Can Help Support the Process

One way principals can help the process of program evaluation go smoothly is to build their own and staff knowledge about it (Howard, 2004). Howard lists some possible resources:

- **Literature on evaluation.** Books, articles, Web sites, and "how to" handbooks may include tips that can make some of your tasks easier.
- **School staff.** Often, you can find previously unidentified expertise in a school that might be helpful to conducting an evaluation.
- **Communication with peers.** You may want to ask other principals/administrators how they conducted a program evaluation. What did they learn? Were there any pitfalls? How did they manage the time commitment?
- **Universities/colleges of education.** If you are located near a college of education, it might be helpful to ask whether a faculty member might be interested, or whether your program evaluation could be used as a student project (2004, p. 33).

In Howard's opinion, principals can also be pivotal in creating "evaluation-friendly" environments in their schools and offers some guidelines:

- Work to help staff understand that the intent is to evaluate programs, not people.
- Ask program planners how they plan to evaluate the success of the program and to routinely build plans for evaluation into every program.
- Integrate data collection into existing procedures as much as possible. This will limit evaluation-related disruptions.
- Coordinate data collection procedures so that multiple evaluation questions can be answered.
- Make it clear that not all program evaluations need to be broad-based. Some important questions can be addressed quite easily (2004, p. 68).

Howard also suggests that you take some time after the evaluation to evaluate *it*. For example,

> If the results of the evaluation did not provide helpful information, then take some time to analyze how this happened. Perhaps critical data was unexpectedly unavailable—or perhaps there were flaws in the design of the evaluation. If the latter is true, it is especially important to identify problems and ways to ensure these will not happen again during another evaluation (2004).

Champion stresses that it is more important that your initial efforts to conduct more systematic reviews of your school's programs be of high quality—even if that means they are fairly limited in scope:

> Think big, but take some small, carefully considered steps. Start with a conversation with your colleagues about what would be most useful to know with some certainty…. You don't need to do everything at once (2004).

# Notes, Reminders, and Ideas:

_____

_____

_____

_____

_____

_____

_____

_____

_____

_____

_____

_____

_____

_____

_____

_____

_____

_____

_____

_____

_____

_____

_____

_____

_____

_____

# Notes, Reminders, and Ideas:

# Chapter 7
# Response to Intervention (RTI) and Data Use

*What are you looking for?*
*How will you look for it?*
*How will you use the data?*

---

*"Response to intervention is a dynamic problem-solving process in which data are integral in making decisions about what skills struggling readers lack, and whether intervention instruction provided has been effective"* (Hall, 2008, p. 17).

---

Viewed from the perspective of broad goals, Response to Intervention (RTI) is intended to ensure that low-performing students receive support in a timely manner. Procedures embedded in RTI:

> begin by ensuring that the general education classroom is providing effective instruction and assessment for all students. RTI then offers a way to bridge gaps between general and special education services by providing scientifically based interventions quickly and efficiently for all students who need support, before going through a lengthy process to determine eligibility for special education (Brown-Chidsey, 2007).

In a jointly-issued white paper, the National Association of State Directors of Special Education and the Council of Administrators of Special Education describe RTI as "the practice of providing high-quality instruction and interventions matched to student need, monitoring progress frequently to make decisions about changes in instruction or goals, and applying child response data to important educational decisions" (2006, p. 2).

Walser characterizes it as "at once simple and complex" (2007). She goes on to talk about its use in one elementary school:

> Four years ago, Callender's school, the Haggerty School in Cambridge, Mass., began a new approach to reading instruction [RTI] when it received a federal Reading First grant. . . All K–3 students in the school are tested for critical prereading and reading skills in the fall, winter, and spring. Students who score in the "some risk" or "at risk" categories are scheduled for intensive interventions to help them catch up. Student progress is recorded on graphs and discussed in monthly meetings. Depending on the results, children may be reassigned to different groups for different kinds of interventions, with schedules changing accordingly.

> Despite the complicated logistics, Callender says the new approach is worth it. "Before, there was only one plan all year, no matter what," the 17-year veteran recalls. "In June there would always be four to five kids who hadn't made the kind of progress I knew they could. I wondered, why am I always missing this same 20%?"

> What was missing were alternatives for these children. At some point in the day, Callender's ten troubled readers will be pulled out of the class to work one-on-one with a specialist or in small groups for more reading practice. Some have learning disabilities, some don't. With RTI, Callender says, there are no more end-of-the-year surprises (2007).

While the initial emphasis of RTI is on successfully addressing the instructional needs of as many students as possible in the regular classroom—and without going through the process of establishing eligibility for special education before students can receive more intensive instruction, some students will need special education services. However, RTI can help with this process as well, as "it can provide schools with much-needed help to better distinguish between the truly disabled and those who might seem to need special education, but who really don't" (Fuchs in Walser, 2007).

Many of the key features of RTI have been in use in schools for over two decades. Educators may recognize both the features and names such as Pre-Referral Intervention Model, Mainstream Assistance Team Model, School-Based Consultation Team Model, and Problem-Solving Model (Horowitz, 2005). However, the model has become much more refined, very data-driven, and has "entered the mainstream" (Walser, 2007).

---

**How Does RTI Differ From Prereferral and Building Assistance Teams?**

RTI is a more comprehensive framework for providing instruction, related interventions, and targeted special education for students at risk . . . RTI is a schoolwide process for bringing stronger alignment to the instruction and assessment practices of a school and is generally more proactive and comprehensive than the more reactive and individualized functions of prereferral and child study teams (Mellard & Johnson, 2008, p. 139).

---

Walser talks about reasons behind RTI's swift and substantial movement into schools across the country. First, it was specifically included as a strategy in the Reading First section of NCLB. Then, it "got another boost from the federal government in final regulations issued for the 2004 IDEA, the law governing special education" (2007).

Though the new IDEA regulations fall short of mandating RTI as a method for identifying children with learning disabilities, they say that states "cannot require" the use of IQ tests to diagnose learning disabilities and they permit states to use "alternate methods" such as RTI to identify learning disabilities. To support early intervention, the regulations allow up to 15% of federal special education funds to be used for this purpose in general education classrooms (Walser, 2007).

While RTI has been given special status by IDEA, "RTI is not a special education process but a general education initiative that fits within school improvement efforts" (Canter, Klotz, & Cowan, 2008, p. 12). Therefore, school efforts to implement the process require close collaboration among regular and special education teachers.

## Data Use and RTI

Data use is at the core of the RTI process, since RTI emphasizes "prevention and swift, data-driven intervention as soon as student difficulties are detected" (Martinez & Nellis, 2008, p. 146). This short overview from the North Dakota Department of Public Instruction Web site identifies some key connections between RTI and data use:

> Data-based decision making is infused in all components of an RTI practice. At the screening level, data would be used to make decisions about which students are at risk of their needs not being met. In the progress monitoring stage, data are used to make decisions about effectiveness of interventions. Decisions to increase or decrease levels of intervention within a Tiered Service Delivery Model are based on student performance data. Data are also used to make decisions regarding the fidelity of implementation (n.d.).

Brown-Chidsey describes the tier-based system of educational services on which RTI is built:

- Tier 1 includes universal instruction and assessment of all students—in other words, the general education curriculum. Schools need to ensure that this instruction and assessment are research-based and effective in helping students gain academic proficiency. Success at Tier 1 is defined as the student demonstrating at least the levels of knowledge and skill expected for his or her age and grade.
- Tier 2 includes selected instructional activities and assessments for students who have not achieved at the expected level while participating in Tier 1. An example of Tier 2 intervention is providing 30 minutes a day of additional reading or math instruction to first grade students who have not met grade-level benchmarks. Students receiving Tier 2 support are monitored weekly to learn whether their skills are improving. If their assessment data indicate progress, the students gradually receive less support until they are able to succeed within the general education (Tier 1) program. If they do not make progress after a specified period of Tier 2 instruction, the school either adjusts the students' Tier 2 instruction or refers them to Tier 3.

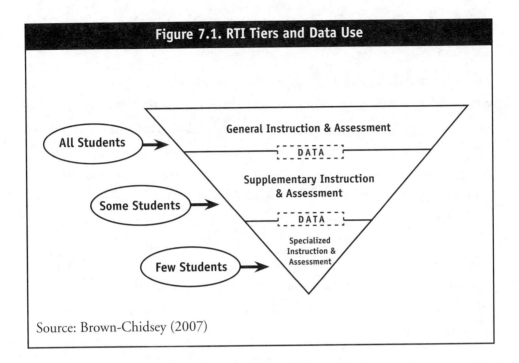

## Figure 7.1. RTI Tiers and Data Use

All Students →
General Instruction & Assessment
DATA

Some Students →
Supplementary Instruction & Assessment
DATA

Few Students →
Specialized Instruction & Assessment

Source: Brown-Chidsey (2007)

• Only at Tier 3 does the school take steps to determine whether a student has a disability that requires special education. At this stage, the school conducts a comprehensive evaluation of the student's skills, including the data obtained in Tiers 1 and 2, to determine why a student's performance is significantly different from that of other students of his or her age and grade and to decide what additional instructional supports the student needs (2007).

In addition, Brown-Chidsey provides a graphic representation of these tiers and of the prominent role data use plays in the system (see Figure 7.1).

RTI *is* an approach for redesigning and establishing teaching and learning environments that are effective, efficient, relevant, and durable for all students, families, and educators.

RTI is *not* a program, curriculum, strategy, or intervention; limited to special education; new (Sugai, 2007).

## What Are You Looking For?

The "what are you looking for?" question in regard to RTI is both very simple and very complex. It is simple because what you will be looking for is: 1) indicators that students are not succeeding and 2) reasons for this lack of success. It is complex because the reasons, in particular, may be difficult to identify. Sometimes, then, the RTI process will move forward by making some educated guesses about what the problem might be and what instructional strategies or supports might help to address this problem.

However, RTI has "guidelines" intended to guard against getting too far off base with these guesses. Specifically, the systematic and frequent reassessment of students receiving differentiated supports provide early indicators of whether the supports are—or are not—helping.

## How Will You Look For It?

Data generation and analysis is at the core of RTI. Johnson, Mellard, Fuchs, and McKnight talk about approaches schools can use to collect data about "the status of students' knowledge, skills, and abilities" (2006). They categorize these into three broad groups: schoolwide screening, diagnostic tests, and progress monitoring procedures and highlight some distinguishing features of the three approaches (see Figure 7.2).

They then go on to talk in more detail about progress monitoring:

> Progress monitoring is a set of assessment procedures for determining the extent to which students are benefiting from classroom instruction and for monitoring effectiveness of curriculum. A fundamental assumption of education is that students will benefit from high-quality instruction. That is, typically, students will learn and achieve the skills and content taught in the classroom. For students who are not responsive to classroom instruction,

| Figure 7.2. Purposes of Three Types of Assessment | | | |
|---|---|---|---|
| | **Screening** | **Progress/ Monitoring** | **Diagnostic Tests** |
| **Population** | Schoolwide | Class/small group/ student | Individual student |
| **Uses** | Broad Index | Specific academic skill or behavioral target | Specific academic domains of knowledge, skills, or abilities |
| **Frequency** | Yearly/3X/monthly | $\leq$ 3 weeks/weekly/daily | Yearly |
| **Purpose** | Identify students who are at risk | Regroup students | Identify specific student deficits |
| **Focus** | School focus | Student/class focus | Student focus |
| **Instruction** | Class/school instruction and curriculum decisions | Within intervention (curriculum/ instruction) | Selecting curriculum and instructional methods |
| **Implications** | As first step for intervention planning | Continue to revise placement | Planning or specifying intervention |

Source: Johnson, Mellard, Fuchs, & McKnight, 2006

alternative interventions can be provided and again the students' response to that instruction can be monitored. Progress monitoring is a valid and efficient tool for gauging the effectiveness of instruction, determining whether instructional modifications are necessary, and providing important information for eventual classification and placement decisions (Johnson, Mellard, Fuchs, & McKnight, 2006).

*"Progress monitoring data inform decisions about when to adjust instruction, when to stay the course, and when to exit a student from intervention"* (Hall, 2008, p. 29).

### Tier 1: Schoolwide Instruction and Student Assessment

In RTI, the continuum of services includes universal interventions at Tier 1, sometimes referred to as "primary prevention," which are in place for all students to support positive academic, behavioral, and mental health outcomes. Tier 1 in RTI involves a high-quality school and classroom environment, scientifically sound core curriculum and instruction, and intentional instructional practices. In Tier 1, school personnel must objectively and systematically evaluate whether their core curriculum materials are of sufficient quality and are backed by research. School staff must also evaluate teachers' instructional methods to make sure their teaching techniques adhere to sound instructional practice and are delivered as intended by the curriculum or intervention program.

To verify whether students are making adequate progress toward basic academic goals, it is imperative to gather data on the population. In Tier 1, schoolwide assessments are conducted to gauge students' performance in the core academic areas (e.g., reading and mathematics). All students are typically assessed three times per year (e.g., fall, winter, and spring) beginning in kindergarten. The purpose of conducting schoolwide assessments is to gather critical data about all students and to identify individuals and groups who are not making satisfactory progress and are at risk for academic or behavioral problems. Students who are not mastering basic academic skills may require additional or different forms of instruction. Systematic reviews of assessment data are often carried out by collaborative instructional support teams, which usually consist of a multidisciplinary team of school personnel such as general and special education teachers, principal, school counselor, school psychologist, and other related services personnel.

### Tier 2: Supplementary Instruction and Progress Monitoring

Tier 2, referred to as "secondary prevention," includes targeted academic and behavioral services for students who are considered at risk and for whom universal instruction was not sufficient. These students were flagged as being at risk through the assessment process. Services at Tier 2 are more intense and are focused on the specific needs of a student or group of students. Examples of services at this second tier might include small group instruction for either academic or behavioral needs, additional support, and involvement in remediation programs such as Title I. Tier 2 interventions are provided to students in addition to the core curriculum.

In addition to the implementation of more targeted, systematic interventions at Tier 2, student progress at Tier 2 is monitored more frequently than it is at Tier 1 (often weekly) to determine student responsiveness to the interventions provided. Typically, those students who respond well to Tier 2 interventions and whose data demonstrate that they are progressing at an acceptable rate (e.g., above the 16th percentile) return to the general education curriculum or intervention offered to all students, or Tier 1. These students continue to participate in the assessment process.

## Tier 3: Intensive Instruction and Continued Progress Monitoring

Despite best efforts in the activities and assessments given at Tiers 1 and 2, some students will continue to struggle. More intensive services may be warranted. The intervention-assessment sequence in Tier 3 is markedly more intensive and individualized, and progress is monitored more frequently than it is in Tier 2. Current best practice in the field suggests that students who do not make adequate progress at Tiers 2 and 3 be further evaluated to rule out conditions such mental retardation and emotional disturbance. Persistent failure to make academic gains at Tiers 2 and 3 may substantiate the presence of a learning disability [Excerpted from Closing the achievement gap series: Part II Response to Intervention (RTI)—Basic elements, practical applications, and policy recommendations. *Education Policy Brief* (Fall 2006). Written by Rebecca S. Martínez, Leah M. Nellis, and Kelly A. Prendergast. Published by Center for Evaluation & Public Policy, Indiana University.]

Hall states: "Why is progress monitoring so important? It is the heart of RTI. These are the data that are used to make adjustments in instruction along the way" (Hall, 2008, p. 82). Curriculum-based measurement (CBM) is considered "the formative assessment method of choice" (Martinez and Nellis, 2008, p. 151). However, other methods can be used to monitor student progress. The Vaughn Gross Center for Reading and Language Arts suggests that educators take the following purposes for progress monitoring into account when selecting approaches; progress monitoring should:

- assess the specific skills embodied in state and local academic standards
- assess marker variables that have been demonstrated to lead to the ultimate instructional target
- be sensitive to small increments of growth over time
- be administered efficiently over short periods
- be administered repeatedly (using multiple forms)
- result in data that can be summarized in teacher-friendly data displays
- be comparable across students
- be applicable for monitoring an individual student's progress over time
- be relevant to development of instructional strategies and use of appropriate curriculum that addresses the area of need (2007, p. 4).

---

**Why RTI Works**

- The strategies and tools are systematic.
- The process is data driven.
- It is based on scientific research and evidence-based solutions.
- It demands problem solving and collaboration.
- It creates solutions to identified problems (Arnberger & Shoop, 2008, p. 54).

---

## How Will You Use the Data?

Obviously, data collection and use under the RTI framework is not a one-time process. School staff members will need to analyze and apply the data to decision making frequently. Establishing a systematic approach to this is important. The National Association of State Directors of Special Education and Council of Administrators of Special Education suggest:

> The use of a structured, problem-solving process is a requisite component of RTI. A structured, systematic problem-solving process assists in the identification of student learning needs and has some basic components. These components include problem identification, analysis of the problem to hypothesize why it is occurring, developing a plan to address the problem, and evaluating the student's response to the intervention/plan selected (2006, p. 5).

It might be helpful to use a practical perspective to frame staff discussion about RTI. For example, the National Center on Learning Disabilities tells educators to:

> think of RTI as a series of steps. The first step is instruction in the general classroom. Screening tests given in the classroom reveal students at risk for reading and other learning difficulties. For example, testing may show that a student who has difficulty reading needs additional instruction in phonics.

> In the second step, the classroom teacher might handle the instruction. In other cases, someone who has expertise in reading and phonics might instruct the student and other students who have the same difficulty.

> Students who fail to respond to this instruction may then be considered for more specialized instruction in step three, where instruction may occur with greater frequency or duration. If the achievement difficulties persist, a team of educators from different fields (for example, reading or counseling) may complete a comprehensive evaluation to determine eligibility for special education and related services (n.d.).

The challenge for school staff members is to identify both the "step" at which a student should be placed and instructional strategies that, when used in that setting, can help the student achieve success. The process is also cyclical, stepping back periodically to review new assessment results to see whether the "right" approach has been selected (Linan-Thompson, Vaughn, Prater, & Cirino, 2006). Tweaking the approach or moving to another one can be a next step if the student still fails to experience success.

> *"While data, graphs, assessment results, and effective tools all make up a substantial part of progress monitoring, the most significant piece is the classroom teacher. It is often said that data drive instruction. If that were true, there would be no need for progress monitoring—the data would select the appropriate instruction, and monitoring for growth would not be necessary. The truth is that the teachers drive the instruction while the data help to guide them"* (Vaughn Gross Center for Reading and Language Arts, 2007, p. 4).

Horowitz talks about the use of data to monitor a student's status as part of the progress monitoring components of RTI:

> Data are collected to document how well students respond to targeted instruction; this in turn guides decisions about how to adjust classroom instruction and whether a formal referral for special education assessment is warranted (2005).

In addition, IDEA now states that data from progress monitoring can also be used as an alternative to use of the "discrepancy model" to determine whether a student is eligible for special education services; specifically,

> Schools are allowed to use evidence of a student's failure to respond to instructional interventions as part of the data documenting the presence of a specific learning disability (Brown-Chidsey, 2007).

## The Principal's Role

So far, the focus in this chapter has been on the details of the process of RTI and on the potential it has for improving all students' opportunities for educational success; however, it is important to recognize that the process will initially require more time, much collaboration, and generate some frustration when instructional approaches do not work. In addition, some teachers may initially experience discomfort with the process since it focuses in a very public way on students who are not experiencing success in their classrooms.

Dealing with all these aspects of RTI implementation—administrative details such as scheduling along with sometimes more difficult issues such as teacher confidence—will require leadership, patience, and, often, some creativity.

An educator interviewed as part of a National Research Center on Learning Disabilities (NRCLD) research project talked about his school's implementation of RTI:

> As we have implemented the RTI process it has continued to be an ongoing challenge at times with staff to have them understand their role and responsibility in the process. And so we continue to go back to data—having data drive our discussion so that we get the feeling side out and get the data side in to help them see that this is about helping the child—it's not evaluating whether they're a good or bad instructor or that it's being perceived that way. But it's about finding the right match, for the right child to get the right intervention started. So, is it easy? No. Is it a long-term process? Yes (n.d.).

Finally, Hall suggests that you "build your base of support around RTI as the right thing to do, not the required thing to do" (2008, p. 21).

---

*"RTI is not a program or a specific strategy, but a prevention framework whose beneficial features should add up to better results"* (Crockett & Gillespie, 2008).

---

## Response to Intervention: Using Data to Analyze Problems and Look for Instructional Solutions

Analyze the Problem—Points to Consider: Look at the problem as the difference between what is expected and what occurs. Analyze the problem with respect to the characteristics of the environment, instruction, curriculum, and the individual learner. Other questions may include:

- Is the instruction delivered with fidelity?
- Is the student missing tool skills (alterable)?
- How is the information provided during instruction?
- What are the characteristics of the learning environment?
- How is the curriculum organized?
- What has not worked in the past?
- What has worked in the past?

Based on the data you have collected, why do you think the problem is occurring?

_____

_____

_____

_____

_____

_____

**Develop a Plan**

Goal: Write a meaningful, measurable, observable goal. Include the conditions (time frame, materials, setting), student's name, behavior, and criterion.

_____

_____

_____

_____

_____

_____

Identify Potential Interventions: Generate a list of interventions. Evaluate each one keeping in mind the research base and record the top six. Place an asterisk (*) by the intervention methods(s) selected for implementation.

1. _____

2. _____

3. _____

4. _____

5. _____

6. _____

(Bergeson, Heuschel, Harmon, Gill, Alig, & Middling, 2006)

# Notes, Reminders, and Ideas:

# Chapter 8

# Using Teacher Observation Data to Improve Instruction

*What are you looking for?*
*How will you look for it?*
*How will you use the data?*

---

*"Observing teachers as they practice their craft provides the most fundamental connection between the instructional leader's role in overseeing the educational program and the teacher's role in implementing that program"* (Williams, Cray, Millen, & Protheroe, 2002).

---

One of a principal's most important responsibilities is ensuring that quality teaching occurs in every classroom. Student performance on required end of the year assessments is one source of data about the quality of instruction. But waiting until the end of the year would mean many months of missed opportunities to help teachers improve their instructional skills. The once-a-year checklist observations of teachers used by many districts for evaluation purposes also suffer from the "too little, too late" problem.

More frequent and targeted classroom visits, on the other hand, can provide valuable information about what happens in classrooms on a day-to-day basis. When followed up by feedback to and conversations with teachers, principals have a powerful tool to improve instruction. Williams, Cray, Millen, and Protheroe view teacher observations as:

an essential means of enhancing the professional knowledge and skills of teachers and building their confidence to meet the needs of diverse learners. Rather than single, isolated events, teacher observations should be a regular part of the professional working environment, seamlessly integrated with the overall professional development process (2002, p. 14).

They also provide a framework that contrasts what they call the traditional and new paradigms of teacher observations and suggest that the new paradigm better addresses today's "challenges of creating and sustaining a high-performing teaching and learning environment" (p. 18) (See Figure 8.1).

The National Association of Elementary School Principals (NAESP) recognizes the importance of teacher observation, as well as the principal's responsibility for it:

Effective principals spend large amounts of time in classrooms, observing the teaching of academic units and provide detailed feedback regarding how teachers' effectiveness can be improved. The point of principal and peer observations is not to catch a teacher doing something wrong. The point is to ensure that all students are meaningfully engaged, actively learning, and that teachers are not simply presenting material.

An important part of classroom observations is to evaluate the instructional skills of individual teachers, to assist these teachers in improving those skills and to help them grow professionally. Collaboration with other teachers and assignment of a mentor may be strategies a principal suggests to assist the teacher, but the conversation often begins between principal and teacher.

School leaders support teachers' professionalism by sharing feedback with teachers about objectives of lessons, the degree of student engagement and the behavior of students.

For new principals in particular, it is essential to be active and involved in the classroom as a dependable presence in the student learning process. Through such involvement, the principal can help teachers instill a sense of success for all students—a feeling that is vastly important to improved student performance (NAESP, 2001, p. 33).

| Figure 8.1. Traditional and New Paradigms for Teacher Observation | |
|---|---|
| **Traditional Paradigm** | **New Paradigm** |
| Infrequent and brief classroom observations | Frequent observations of varied lessons/practices |
| Focus on student behavior | Focus on student learning |
| Focus on classroom management | Focus on effective teaching |
| Judgments based on personal philosophy and teaching style | Judgments based on evidence of student learning |
| Focus on lesson plans | Focus on curriculum standards and learning objectives |
| "One size fits all" observations | Contextually-appropriate observations |
| Single observation method and protocol is used | Multiple methods and protocols are used |
| Power (supervisory authority) supersedes craft knowledge and expertise | Research-based best practices are the basis of expertise authority |
| Changes in practice based on principal recommendations | Changes in practice based on professional development goals/plans |
| Each observation a discrete event | Observations part of a teacher development process linked to goals and prior observation results |
| Feedback from principal only | Feedback connected to collaborative dialogue with other teachers (Williams, Cray, Millen, & Protheroe, 2002, p. 19) |

In line with the role of instructional leader, the principal is a key part in ensuring that teacher observations are as effective as they can be. To do this aspect of the job well, a principal needs an understanding of standards for student learning, an in-depth sense of what good teaching looks like, and strong communication and interpersonal skills (Protheroe, 2002, p. 5). NAESP recognizes the need to provide training for school leaders in skills such as these. For example, principals need "strong skills in providing open, constructive, and accurate feedback" (2001, p. 25).

NAESP also encourages principals to engage in reflective practice as another means of refining their skills related to teacher observation. For example, they might ask:

- How often am I in classrooms? What evidence do I see of good teaching and high levels of learning?
- What kinds of feedback do I share with teachers after observing their classes? Does this feedback focus on the teacher's lessons, methods of instruction, and student learning? Does it focus on the extent to which all students were engaged in meaningful/relevant instructional activities? How do I use what I learn from students and student work/performance to help teachers improve their practices? (2001, p. 38).

## What Are You Looking For?

To positively impact instruction, there are several aspects of data collection and use that must be carefully structured. Think back to our three key data questions: What are you looking for? How will you look for it? How will you use the data? In planning teacher observations, principals need to carefully define what they are looking for. In this chapter we talk about very specific indicators of good teaching. While these indicators could be part of this "looking for" list, there are three important categories that should be part of your observation plan:

- Teaching to standards,
- Evidence that students are engaged in learning, and
- Instructional strategies identified by research as "good teaching."

## Teaching to Standards

In today's standards-based educational environment, both principals and teachers need a clear understanding of what students are expected to know and be able to do. Marshall states:

> When a principal visits a classroom, one of the most important things to looks for is whether the teacher is on target with the curriculum. Of course, to answer the question means that the principal must know what exactly the curriculum is... Teacher supervision can't be efficient and effective until curriculum expectations are clear and widely accepted within the school (Marshall, 2003, p. 705).

Many districts have worked to develop curricula carefully aligned with their standards. In addition, pacing guides may have been developed. These curriculum guides and—even more important—the pacing guides provide roadmaps for elements of instruction principals should observe while in classrooms.

These roadmaps are especially helpful when visiting the classroom of a teacher whose students are demonstrating less progress than those of another teacher working at the same grade level or teaching the same content. If your teachers have pacing guides available to them, familiarize yourself with the content that should be taught during the general time period of your visit. Do you see a lesson that focuses on teaching this content? If not, talk with the teacher about the reasons why. Is he or she having difficulty keeping students' progress on track? If so, some assistance for the teacher—or for some students experiencing difficulty and therefore slowing down progress—might be needed. Your follow-up support might focus on providing opportunities for the teacher to observe in another classroom. Or perhaps the grade level teachers could meet together to discuss ways to better support low-performing students. Another explanation might be that the teacher pays too little attention to the pacing guide—instead continuing in familiar patterns such as teaching to the textbook. This also requires your attention.

## Figure 8.2. Monitoring, Assessment, and Follow-Up

### 4—Expert

The teacher:
- Posts the criteria for proficient work, including rubrics and exemplars, and students internalize them.
- Uses a variety of first-rate assessments to prediagnose and continuously monitor students' learning.
- Continuously checks for understanding, unscrambles confusion, and gives specific, helpful feedback.
- Has students set ambitious goals, self-assess and monitor, and take responsibility for their progress.
- Frequently posts students' work with rubrics and commentary and uses it to motivate and direct effort.
- Immediately uses interim assessment data to fine-tune teaching, re-teach, and help struggling students.
- Relentlessly follows up with struggling students with time and support to reach proficiency.
- Makes sure that students who need specialized diagnosis and help receive appropriate services ASAP.
- Charts and analyzes assessment data, draws action conclusions, and shares them with others.
- Constantly reflects on the effectiveness of teaching and works every day to improve.

### 3—Proficient

- Posts clear criteria for proficiency, including rubrics and exemplars of student work.
- Diagnoses students' knowledge and skills up front and uses a variety of assessments during each unit.
- Frequently checks for understanding and gives students helpful feedback if they seem confused.
- Has students set goals, self-assess, and know where they stand academically at all times.
- Regularly posts students' work to make visible and celebrate their progress with respect to standards.
- Uses data from interim assessments to adjust teaching, reteach, and follow up with failing students.
- Takes responsibility for students who are not succeeding and tenaciously gives them extra help.
- When necessary, refers students for specialized diagnosis and extra help.

- Analyzes data from summative assessments, draws conclusions, and shares them appropriately.
- Reflects on the effectiveness of lessons and units and continuously works to improve them.

2—Needs Improvement

- Tells students some of the qualities that their finished work should exhibit.
- Uses pencil-and-paper quizzes and tests with some open-ended questions to assess student learning.
- Asks questions to see if students understand.
- Urges students to look over their tests, see where they had trouble, and aim to improve those areas.
- Posts some 'A' student work as an example for others.
- Looks over students' tests to see if there is anything that needs to be retaught.
- Offers students who fail tests some additional time to study and do retakes.
- Sometimes doesn't refer students promptly for special help, or refers students who don't need it.
- Records students' grades and notices some general patterns for future reference.
- At the end of a teaching unit or semester, thinks about what might have been done better.

1—Does Not Meet Standards

- Expects students to know (or figure out) what it takes to get good grades.
- Uses only multiple-choice and short-answer pencil-and-paper tests to assess student learning.
- Rarely takes time to check for understanding.
- Urges students to work harder and be more careful on future tests.
- Posts only a few samples of 'A' work.
- Looks over unit and final tests to see if there are any lessons for the future.
- Tells students that if they fail a test, that's it; the class has to move on to cover the curriculum.
- Either fails to refer students for special education or refers students who do not need it.
- Records students' grades and moves on with the curriculum.
- When a teaching unit or lesson doesn't go well, chalks it up to experience.

Overall rating: ___ Comments:

Source: Marshall, K. (2006b). Teacher evaluation rubrics: The why and the how. *EDge Magazine* (September/October 2006).

## Evidence That Students Are Engaged in Learning

Every principal has gone into classrooms that are vibrant examples of students engaged in learning—and into classrooms in which students' attention is wandering. This is another indicator that should be part of your observations. Does the teacher make use of a variety of approaches—whole class as well as small group, encouraging responses from all students, etc.—that generate student participation and enthusiasm? Keep in mind, though, that a "fun" classroom also needs to be standards-based. Students should be engaged in learning the "right stuff," in content that will provide help to their efforts to meet standards, not simply responding to good teaching strategies.

## Instructional Strategies Identified as "Good Teaching"

Research is providing an increasingly strong base of information—written in practitioner-relevant language—about good teaching strategies. Protheroe talks about the need for principals to be knowledgeable about this:

> For the teacher observation process to be effective, the principal needs a solid foundation of knowledge about good teaching. The research base on effective teaching suggests components that principals should look for as they conduct observations. It also serves as a powerful foundation for principal-teacher conversations about good teaching, provides a resource for teachers who are working to strengthen their skills, and guides planning for professional development (2002, p. 4).

Marshall (2006b) describes his efforts to develop a rubric-based system for teacher observation that focused on key elements of a teacher's responsibilities, provides clear descriptions of teacher behaviors, and could be easily used by teachers and principals as a basis for discussion. Figure 8.2 is the observation sheet he developed for the domain of Monitoring, Assessment, and Follow up. This sheet—along with others covering the domains of Planning and Preparation for Teaching, Classroom Management, Delivery of Instruction, Family and Community Outreach, and Professional Responsibilities—would be used to as an "end-of- year evaluation based on numerous short, informal, unannounced classroom visits, each followed up with a face-to-face conversation with the teacher" (email communication with Kim Marshall, February 26, 2008). A teacher might exhibit some behaviors classified as expert, while other behaviors might fall in other categories. This rubric sheet—which Marshall highlights to indicate what he observed—provides a roadmap to areas for teacher improvement.

## How Will You Look For It?

Most school districts have a structure for required teacher observations. Many of them are checklist based, and some differentiate between new and experienced teachers. However, many—if not most—of these required approaches have two significant shortcomings. They happen so seldom that they may allow less-than-effective teaching practices to continue through an entire school year, and they are not explicitly tied to principal-teacher conversations that result in individualized teacher development opportunities. Thus, such systems are unlikely to result in a strong follow-up plan for teacher development.

On a positive note, many educators are recognizing the role that effective teacher observation can play in helping teachers continually grow and improve their performance. Stansbury (2001) suggests that teacher observation should be embedded in the day-to-day work of professional growth and classroom practice. As principal you should ask yourself "Is the approach I am using for teacher observation—or one I am thinking about using—designed to help teachers strengthen their abilities to teach all students to high standards?"

Teacher observation to improve performance requires greater skill on the part of principals than did traditional, checklist-based observation systems, but this kind of teacher observation can yield substantial benefits that are worth the effort. By forging a strong and clear link between teacher observation and teacher development, you take an important step toward the goal of ensuring a high-performing teacher in every classroom.

Kaplan and Owings (2001) provide guidelines principals might use when redesigning their approach to teacher observation and follow-up:

- Make teaching effectiveness and working closely with teachers in classroom observations and conferencing a priority.
- Vigorously seek instructional best practices in all classroom observations and teacher conferences.
- Visit all classrooms frequently for at least 10 minutes and look for instructional best practices even when they are not part of a formal summative assessment.
- Give teachers specific, positive feedback about what was observed.

Williams, Cray, Millen, and Protheroe also stress that any framework for an observation system should take teachers' individual professional needs into account. The purposes for conducting a specific teacher observation—or series of observations—could include the following:

- **Intervening to rectify a problem**—Expectations for instruction or the appropriate treatment of students are not being met.
- **Coaching to improve**—The teacher is working to refine a specific practice or deal more effectively with a particular situation.
- **Monitoring the implementation of a program or component of a model**—The principal wants to ensure that the program is being implemented as intended (fidelity).
- **Responding to a teacher's request for assistance in handling a particular situation**—The teacher wants suggestions for learning strategies to achieve a specific learning goal or work with a particular type of student.
- **Affirming and reinforcing**—The principal supports the teacher's growth, effectiveness, or success in implementing a new practice.
- **Documenting and recording**—The observer records specific techniques or documents examples of student learning.

These are not discrete purposes; in practice they overlap. The point is that in planning the observation, the principal should have a clear purpose that can be communicated to the teacher and used to prepare, implement, and follow-up on the observation (2002, p. 26-27).

Williams, Cray, Millen, and Protheroe also stress that principals should keep in mind other factors—other characteristics—that might vary among teachers in the school:

Accepting diversity in a staff means recognizing that teachers differ in their ability to examine their own practices and in their openness to having others examine their work. They also differ in the readiness, knowledge, skills, and orientations they bring to the teaching and learning process. Principals must approach the observer role with the same appreciation for teacher diversity that they expect teachers to recognize in their students. This requires a range of observation strategies that are responsive to the differentiated needs of a diverse staff (2002, p. 11-12).

## Some Approaches to Teacher Observation

From a structural standpoint, each observation "system" should take into account planning for three phases:

- Pre-observation—during which you decide what you will be looking for and communicate this to the teacher(s);
- Observation; and
- Post-observation feedback to the teacher.

Marshall (1996) talks about his personal evolution toward a new approach to teacher observation while he worked as a principal. After becoming increasingly dissatisfied with the information that his district's more formal observations process provided him about teacher knowledge, skills, and performance, he began to add 5 minute visits to classrooms to his everyday schedule, eventually finding that he could manage four or five visits a day. Marshall used these guidelines as he developed his approach to visiting classroom:

- Classroom visits would have to be brief (otherwise they couldn't be frequent and still fit into my hectic schedule) but not *too* brief (because then I'd fail to see what was really going on).
- Visits would have to be frequent; otherwise there wouldn't be enough of them to balance specific praise with specific criticism.
- Visits would have to be random and unannounced, or I would risk seeing only specially prepared, glamorized lessons.

- I would need to give feedback soon after every visit, or teachers would be left guessing about conclusions I had drawn.
- The feedback should be presented face to face to make it as nonthreatening as possible and to allow for conversation about what was happening in the classroom (1996, p. 339).

Marshall provided feedback to each of the teachers visited—ideally, by the end of the same day. In his view, these visits helped to enrich his relationships with teachers and to build his knowledge of both curriculum and instruction in his school.

Neide (1996) talks about periodically focusing on a very narrow range of teacher behaviors when making short classroom visits. She suggests observing and documenting how a teacher interacts with students—for example, what types of positive and negative feedback are provided—can be the purpose of an observation.

Peery talks about her use of a transcription process for longer observations as a supplement to the district-supplied checklist-type teacher observation form. She uses these transcripts to jumpstart conversations with teachers:

> I let the teacher's comments guide the conversation unless there is something I was alarmed about, such as student safety, blatant disregard for school procedures, or curriculum and instruction practices I could not support.

> Teachers notice things in my transcripts that I would never see: improvements they want to make in a lesson, for example….The transcripts and conversations then provide the impetus for inquiry (2002, p. 26).

## How Will You Use the Data?

Follow-up from a classroom observation deserves careful attention. In Van der Linde's view, "The follow-up discussion sometimes provides the most important situation for the collection of further data, because teachers are now in a situation where they are able to explain their behavior" (1998, p. 332).

**Peery's Transcription Process**

- Be a careful observer. Write down all you see and hear for a period of at least 30 minutes or one complete class activity. Be sure to note facial expressions, body language, and actual words spoken by the teacher and the students. Note the time in the margins periodically.
- Provide the transcript to the teacher within 24 hours. Type it after the observation if it's not legible . . . or provide a photocopy.
- Invite or require the teacher to confer with you as follow-up.... Allow the teacher to choose the time of the conference unless you have fairly serious concerns. If you have serious concerns, schedule the conference as soon as possible which could be at the end of the class period or during the teacher's lunch the same day, if necessary.
- In the conference, ask the teacher, "What did you see in the transcript? What is worthy of discussion?" If possible, let the teacher lead the discussion. This is where the real learning takes place. Plan for ongoing follow-up.
- For a teacher you have some concerns about, arrange a longer follow-up visit. Allow the teacher to pick the date and time and look for improvements in things that you and the teacher have already discussed.
- Confer after this observation and conduct an unannounced one shortly afterwards as well. Continue the cycle of observations and conferences until the problems you noted are under control or you decide to take some other action (Peery 2002, p. 27).

*"The key to success as a clinical supervisor is to first understand the teacher's perception of the data and its meaning"* (Pajak, 2001, p. 241).

Marshall talks about conversations he had with teachers as follow-ups to short and frequent visits he made to classrooms:

I found that verbal feedback worked best. When I occasionally gave feedback in a written note or an email, the teacher rarely responded, so there was no dialogue. I also found that I was much more guarded about putting negative feedback in writing because it was more permanent (and more threatening) and because I couldn't judge the teacher's mood and ability to absorb a critical comment. Written feedback also deprived me of the rich and substantive conversations that often grew out of face-to-face feedback talks. So I stuck almost entirely to verbal follow-ups, usually stand-up conversations in such informal settings as the teacher's classroom during a free period, in a corridor, by the copy machine, or while walking to our cars after school. These talks lasted an average of 3 to 5 minutes…. The feedback conversations played an important ethical role in this system: they gave teachers a chance to clue me in on the broader context of a particular teaching moment, to correct me if I misheard or got the wrong idea, and to push back if they disagreed with a criticism (2003, p. 704).

He also is clear that principals need to provide objective, truthful feedback to teachers they observe:

Some principals sugarcoat criticism and give inflated scores for fear of hurting feelings. This does not help teachers improve. The kindest thing a principal can do for an underperforming teacher is to give candid, evidence-based feedback and robust follow-up support (Marshall, 2008, p. 1).

Glanz considers feedback an integral part of the observation process, and he adds an interesting thought for principals to keep in mind:

Observation is a two-step process: first, to describe what has occurred, and second, to interpret what it means. Too often, we jump into what has been termed the *interpretation trap*. We jump to conclusions about a particular behavior before describing that behavior. When we interpret first, we not only lose description of the event, but also create communication difficulties that might result in teacher resistance (2004, p. 48).

Obviously, translating your observations into opportunities for teacher development is also important. Williams, Cray, Millen, and Protheroe talk about the link between observation and professional development: "We have traditionally viewed teacher observation as but one strategy for supporting teacher development; we now must think of it as the foundation for teacher development" (2002, p. 14).

Holland reminds principals to make the link between teacher formative evaluation—in particular, observations that together contribute to the data base needed for evaluation—and teacher development explicit. These observations should be used to "identify a teacher's current levels of knowledge and skill and use them as the basis for a coherent and documented plan for that teacher's continued learning and professional development" (2005, p. 72).

Supports you offer teachers might include resource materials, peers who can serve as coaches or who themselves can be observed, professional development programs, courses, or independent projects such as action research.

> *"The observation process should be embedded in the overall professional development process, with clear connections to long-term development goals. The instructional leader's approach is based on this central question: 'What is the best approach for helping this teacher learn and enhance his or her practice given the learning goals for students, given this teacher in this situation?'"* (Williams, Cray, Millen, & Protheroe, 2002, p. 45).

## Introducing a New Approach to Classroom Observation

For teachers accustomed to annual, checklist-driven approaches to classroom observation, a move to more frequent, often-unannounced principal visits may be seen as a major shift in practice. Williams, Cray, Millen, and Protheroe discuss the need for principals to address such considerations:

Changing any process within the school requires careful planning based on many factors. Modifying the teacher observation process is no exception; indeed, because it focuses on one of the most private aspects of schooling—what goes on behind the closed doors of classrooms—these factors can be quite complex. In some schools, these changes involve relatively minor shifts in a teacher observation and instructional improvement process that is well accepted. In other settings, however, introducing a teacher observation process aimed at improving instructional practice and student learning represents a major organizational change that involves substantial changes in the culture of the school (2002, p. 39).

Finally, your approach to conducting classroom observation and providing feedback should be perceived as a challenge, not a threat, to teachers. How you communicate the process—in actions as well as words—can significantly impact teachers' willingness to view it as a positive support for their own professional improvement.

# Notes, Reminders, and Ideas:

_____

_____

_____

_____

_____

_____

_____

_____

_____

_____

_____

_____

_____

_____

_____

_____

_____

_____

_____

_____

_____

_____

_____

_____

_____

# Notes, Reminders, and Ideas:

_____

_____

_____

_____

_____

_____

_____

_____

_____

_____

_____

_____

_____

_____

_____

_____

_____

_____

_____

_____

_____

_____

_____

_____

_____

# Chapter 9
# Summing Up

*"Effective leaders are skilled at focusing on the most important data and bringing it to the forefront so it can be analyzed to inform changes that make sense for the school's staff and community"* (National Association for Elementary School Principals, 2008, p. 99).

Just a few examples of ways in which data use can support school improvement efforts have been presented in this resource. You and your staff could probably brainstorm dozens more in just a few minutes. Remember that such endeavors need not be "big" projects. Many times the data question can focus on a small and manageable concern. However, addressing this small concern through careful study can often have big payoffs. Here are some additional examples of ways your school might use data.

Ask new teachers how things are going—but in an organized way. Focus on things they feel are particularly helpful in providing them with support, as well as on things they see as barriers. Then use this "data" to identify ways you and the rest of the staff can provide stronger support for these new teachers.

New teachers can be encouraged to assess their own use of instructional strategies by paying special attention to a few students. They should ask themselves: Are these students engaged or not? Have they all demonstrated understanding of instructions and assignments? Are there lessons that seem to go especially well for them—or not so well? Spending time with a new teacher to talk about how to structure these observations and then to discuss what they felt these observations told them can help to improve instruction while building data analysis skills.

Helping students learn how to use data to support their own learning is another application of data use and analysis. For example, Gregory and Kuzmich (2004) suggest that students be encouraged to self-assess their work using teacher-provided rubrics—then use the "data" they collect to improve.

One elementary school uses a graphic display of data to help generate questions intended to help keep children's progress on track. Hundreds of color-coded cards grouped by grade level line the "Assessment Wall" in the office of the school's literacy coordinator. Each card represents a student (names on the back for privacy purposes) and his/her progress through assessment STEPS (Strategic Teaching and Evaluation of Progress). Teachers meet twice a month with the coordinator to review status and progress, "group and regroup pupils according to the progress they are making, identify pupils who are reading below grade level, and—most importantly—exchange intervention strategies to help those who are struggling" (Pardini, 2000).

One final example—A principal concerned about the amount of whole-class, teacher-directed instruction he was seeing during his classroom visits decided to include teachers in the observation process. Time that had been set aside for professional development was reallocated to having teachers do "multiple pop-in visits to as many classrooms as they could reasonably visit in one class period" (McEnery, 2005, p. 45). Teachers were asked to use an observation form provided by the principal to record what they observed teachers and students doing. After pulling together and sharing data from these multiple observations, the principal provided time for teachers to discuss their observations. In his view, the observations and the resulting discussions provided "motivation for change" (p. 46), with teachers asking for professional development focused on use of less teacher-directed strategies.

Earl and Katz (2006) see effective data use as an important element of professional learning communities. In such schools, educators collaborate to problem solve, a setting the authors characterize as a "culture of inquiry." An important role for principals is helping teachers and other staff members develop an "inquiry habit of mind." They need to feel comfortable with having the sometimes difficult discussions focused on problems identified through data use and consider themselves capable of identifying solutions to these.

> *"Clearly, data analysis is not a panacea that will solve every problem in a school. But when properly focused and implemented, data analysis is one tool that a school's staff can use to help raise educational achievement"* (Wade, 2001, p. 2).

Earlier in this book, it was stressed that some "necessary prior conditions" must be in place if a school is to move forward with systematic data use for improvement. Some of these—such as time for teachers to work together—can be made available on an ad hoc basis around a specific project. Others, in particular an environment of trust, need to be in place long before data is used to evaluate a program or to focus teachers on each other's work through the RTI process. Ensuring these conditions are met will fall primarily on the principal's shoulders.

In addition, principals should take the lead in demonstrating the value of data use to school improvement. Boudett and Steele talk about the importance of this:

> Challenging as it is, using data to improve teaching and learning is possible. In our experience, the key lies in building a school culture in which faculty members collaborate regularly and make instructional decisions based on evidence about students' skills and understanding (2007, p. 2).

They also talk about the first step—Prepare—of the Data Wise process, a cyclical approach to data use for school improvement. In this phase,

> School leaders typically face two critical challenges: communicating the need for a data initiative and creating data teams that are equipped to lead the work. The leaders we studied confront these challenges in two ways: by making data relevant, and by giving their data teams time to develop the skills and systems they need to be successful (2008, p. 1).

Finally, while data use can provide a critical support for school improvement efforts, it must be accompanied with hard, focused work since "the leap from data to action is not simple" (Knapp, Swinnerton, Copland, & Monpas-Huber, 2007, p. 18). As school leader, perhaps the most difficult—and most necessary—part of your job is ensuring that this work happens.

# Notes, Reminders, and Ideas:

# References

Aldersebaes, I., Potter, J., & Hamilton, N. (2000). *Programs don't—people do: Insights into schoolwide change*. Portland, OR: Northwest Regional Educational Laboratory.

Arlington Public Schools. (1999). *A framework for systematic accountability and evaluation*. Arlington, VA: Author.

Arnberger, K., & Shoop, R. J. (2008). Responding to need. *Principal Leadership* (January 2008), 51-54.

Aschbacher, P. R., Koency, G., & Schacter, J. (1995). *Los Angeles Learning Center alternative assessment guidebook*. Los Angeles, CA: National Center for Research on Evaluation, Standards, and Student Testing (CRESST).

Bergeson, T., Heuschel, M. A., Harmon, B., Gill, D. H., Alig, P., & Middling, T. (2006). *Using Response to Intervention (RTI) for Washington's students*. Olympia, WA: Washington Office of Superintendent of Public Instruction.

Black, P., & Wiliam, D. (1998). Inside the black box: Raising standards through classroom assessment. *Phi Delta Kappan* (October 1998). Retrieved online from www.pdkintl.org/kappan/kbla9810.htm

Boudett, K., & Moody, L. (2005). Organizing for collaborative work. In K.P. Boudett, E.A. City, & R.J. Murnane (Eds.), *Data Wise: A step-by-step guide to using assessment results to improve teaching and learning*. Cambridge, MA: Harvard Education Press.

Boudett, K. P., & Steele, J. L. (2007). *Data Wise in action*. Cambridge, MA: Harvard Education Press.

Boudett, K.P., & Steele, J.L. (Eds.). (2007). *Data Wise in action: Stories of schools using data to improve teaching and learning*. Cambridge, MA: Harvard University Press.

Brown-Chidsey, R. (2007). No more "waiting to fail": How Response to Intervention works and why it is needed. *Educational Leadership* (October 2007), 40-46.

Canter, A., Klotz, M. B., & Cowan, K. (2008). Response to Intervention: The future for secondary schools. *Principal Leadership* (February 2008), 12-15.

Center for Comprehensive School Reform and Improvement. (2005). *Tools for evaluating school progress*. Retrieved online from http://www.centerforcsri.org/index.php?option=com_content&task=view&id=86&Itemid=79

Center for Comprehensive School Reform and Improvement. (2006). *Program evaluation for the practitioner: Using evaluation as a school improvement strategy*. Washington, DC: Author.

Champion, R. (2002). Choose the right data for the job: A good evaluation measures the same thing from different angles. *Journal of Staff Development* (Summer 2002), 78-79.

Champion, R. (2004). Taking Measure: Frequently asked questions from the evaluator's mailbox. *Journal of Staff Development* (Summer 2004). Retrieved online from www.nsdc.org/library/publications/jsd/champion253.cfm

Cicchinelli, L., & Barley, Z. (1999). *Evaluating for success: Comprehensive school reform: An evaluation guide for districts and schools.* Aurora, CO: Mid-continent Research for Education and Learning.

City, E.A., Kagel, M., & Teoh, M. B. (2005). Examining instruction. In K.P. Boudette, E.A. City, & R.J. Murnane (Eds.). *Data Wise: A step-by-step guide to using assessment results to improve teaching and learning.* Cambridge, MA: Harvard Education Press.

Connecticut Department of Education. (2000). *Connecticut's blueprint for reading achievement: The report of the Early Reading Success Panel.* Retrieved online from www.state.ct.us/sde/dtl/ curriculum/currcbra.htm

Cox, J. (2007). *Finding the story behind the numbers: A tool-based guide for evaluating educational programs.* Thousand Oaks, CA: Corwin Press.

Creighton, T. B. (2007). *Schools and data: The educator's guide for using data to improve decision making* (2nd ed.). Thousand Oaks, CA: Corwin Press.

Crockett, J. B., & Gillespie, D. N. (2008). Getting ready for RTI: A principal's guide to Response to Intervention. *ERS Spectrum 25*(4), 1-9.

Cromey, A., & Hanson, M. (2000). *An exploratory analysis of school-based student assessment systems.* Naperville, IL: North Central Regional Education Laboratory. Retrieved online from http://www.ncrel.org/re/eval/mi/analysis.htm

Damian, C. (2000). Facing—and embracing—the assessment challenge. *ENC Focus 7*(2), 16-17.

Denton, D. R. (1999). *Reading reform in the SREB states: Early assessment.* Atlanta, GA: Southern Regional Education Board.

Depka, E. (2006). *The data guidebook for teachers and leaders: Tools for continuous improvement.* Thousand Oaks, CA: Corwin Press.

Earl, L., & Katz, S. (2006). *Leading schools in a data-rich world: Harnessing data for school improvement.* Thousand Oaks, CA: Corwin Press.

Earl, L. M., & Katz, S. (2008). *Leading schools in a data-rich world (Facilitator's guide).* Thousand Oaks, CA: Corwin Press.

Early Childhood Research Institute on Measuring Growth and Development (1998). *Research and development of individual growth and development indicators for children between birth and age eight* (Tech. Rep. No. 4). Minneapolis, MN: Center for Early Education and Development, University of Minnesota.

FPG Child Development Institute. (2006) Detecting early warning signs in children at risk for learning disabilities. *FPG Snapshot* (June 2006). Retrieved online from http://www. recognitionandresponse.org/images/downloads/resources/randrsnapshot.pdf

Glanz, J. (2004). *The assistant principal's handbook: Strategies for success.* Thousand Oaks, CA: Corwin Press.

Goodman, K. (1973). *Miscue analysis: Applications to reading instruction.* Urbana, IL: NCTE.

Gregory, G. H., & Kuzmich, L. (2004). *Data driven differentiation in the standards-based classroom.* Thousand Oaks, CA: Corwin Press.

Guskey, T. R. (2002). Does it make a difference? Evaluating professional development. *Educational Leadership* (March 2002), 45-51.

Hall, S. (2008). *A principal's guide to implementing Response to Intervention.* Thousand Oaks, CA: Corwin Press.

Hammond, O. (2006). The evaluation corner. *Pacific Educator* (Spring 2006), 11.

Harvey, S., & Goudvis, A. (2000). *Strategies that work: Teaching comprehension to enhance understanding.* York, ME: Stenhouse Publishers.

Heritage, M. & Yeagerly, R. (2005). Data use and school improvement: Challenges and prospects. In J.L. Herman & E.H. Haertel (Eds.), *Uses and misuses of data for educational accountability and improvement.* Malden, MA: Blackwell Publishing.

Herman, J. L., & Winters, L. (1992). *Tracking your school's success: A guide to sensible evaluation.* Newbury Park, CA: Corwin Press.

Holcomb, E. (2004). *Getting excited about data* (2nd ed.). Thousand Oaks, CA: Corwin Press.

Holland, P. (2005). The case for expanding standards for teacher evaluation to include an instructional supervision perspective. *Journal of Personnel Evaluation in Education 18,* 67-77.

Horowitz, S. H. (2005). Response to Intervention: A primer. *LD News* (July 2005). Retrieved online from http://www.ncld.org/index.php?option=content&task=view&id=598

Howard, L. (2004). *Essentials for principals: Effective program evaluation.* Alexandria, VA: National Association of Elementary School Principals and Educational Research Service.

Jandris, T. P. (2001). *Essentials for principals: Data-based decision making.* Alexandria, VA: National Association of Elementary School Principals and Educational Research Service.

Johnson, E., Mellard, D. F., Fuchs, D., & McKnight, M. A. (2006). *Responsiveness to Intervention (RTI): How to do it.* Lawrence, KS: National Research Center on Learning Disabilities. Retrieved online from http://nrcld.org/rti_manual/

Johnson, J. H. (2000). Data-driven school improvement. *Journal of School Improvement* (Spring 2000). Retrieved online from http://www.ncacasi.org/jsi/2000v1i1/data_driven

Johnson, R. S. (2002). *Using data to close the achievement gap: How to measure equity in our schools.* Thousand Oaks, CA: Corwin Press.

Johnston, J., Knight, M., & Miller, L. (2007). Finding time for teams. *Journal of Staff Development* (Spring 2007), 14-18.

Kame'enui, E. J., & Simmons, D. C. (1998). Beyond effective practice to schools as host environments: Building and sustaining a schoolwide intervention model in beginning reading instruction. *OSSC Bulletin* (Spring 1998).

Kaplan, L. S., & Owings, W. A. (2001). Teacher quality and student achievement: Recommendations for principals. *NASSP Bulletin* (November 2001). Retrieved online from www.principals.org/news/bltn_tch_qul_stdnt_ach1101.htm

Kaufman, R., Guerra, I., & Platt, W. A. (2006). *Practical evaluation for educators: Finding what works and what doesn't.* Thousand Oaks, CA: Corwin Press.

Killion, J. (2002). *Assessing impact: Evaluating staff development.* Oxford, OH: National Staff Development Council.

Killion, J., & Bellamy, G. T. (2000). On the job: Data analysts focus school improvement efforts. *Journal of Staff Development* (Winter 2000). retrieved online from http://www.nsdc.org/educatorindex.htm

Knapp, M. A., Swinnerton, J. A., Copland, M.A., & Monpas-Huber, J. (2006) *Data-informed leadership in education: A research report in collaboration with the Wallace Foundation.* Seattle, WA: Center for the Study of Teaching and Policy, University of Washington. Retrieved online from http://depts.washington.edu/ctpmail/PDFs/DataInformed-Nov1.pdf

Langer, G. M., Colton, A. B., & Goff, L. (2003). *Collaborative analysis of student work: Improving teaching and learning.* Alexandria, VA: Association of Supervision and Curriculum Development.

Learning First Alliance. (2000). *Every child reading: A professional development guide.* Retrieved online from www.learningfirst.org/readingguide.html

Linan-Thompson, S., Vaughn, S., Prater, K., and Cirino, P. T. (2006). The Response to Intervention of English language learners at risk for reading problems. *Journal of Reading Disabilities* (September/October 2006), 390-398.

Lyon, G. R. (1998). Overview of reading and literacy research. In S. Patton & M. Holmes (Eds.), *The Keys to Literacy.* Washington, DC: Council for Basic Education.

Lyon, G. R. (1997). *Statement made before the Committee on Education and the Workforce.* U.S. House of Representatives, July 10, 1999, Washington, DC.

Marshall, K. (1996). How I confronted HSPS (Hyperactive Superficial Principal Syndrome) and began to deal with the heart of the matter. *Phi Delta Kappan* (January 1996), 336-345.

Marshall, K. (2003). Recovering from HSPS (Hyperactive Superficial Principal Syndrome): A progress report. *Phi Delta Kappan* (May 2003), 701-709.

Marshall, K. (2006a). *Interim assessments: Keys to successful implementation.* New York: New Leaders for New Schools. Retrieved online from http://www.marshallmemo.com/articles/Interim%20Assmt%20Report%20Apr.%2012,%2006.pdf

Marshall, K. (2006b). Teacher evaluation rubrics: The why and the how. *EDge Magazine* (September/October 2006). Retrieved from http://www.marshallmemo.com/articles/EDge%20Rubrics%20Jan.%2025,%2006.doc

Martinez, R. S., & Nellis, L. M. (2008). Response to Intervention: A school-wide approach for promoting academic wellness for all students. In B. Doll and J.A. Cummings (Eds.), *Transforming School Mental Health Services* (pp. 143-164). Thousand Oaks, CA: Corwin Press.

Martinez, R. S., Nellis, L. M., & Prendergast, K. A. (2006). Closing the achievement gap series: Part II Response to Intervention (RTI)—Basic elements, practical applications, and policy recommendations. *Education Policy Brief* (Fall 2006). Retrieved online from http://ceep.indiana.edu/projects/PDF/PB_V4N8_Fall_2006_AchievementGap.pdf

McAfee, O., Leong, D., & Bodrova, E. (2004). *Basics of assessment: A primer for early childhood educators.* Washington, DC: National Association for the Education of Young Children.

McEnery, D. (2005). Getting out of the way: A lesson in change. *Principal Leadership* (May 2005), 42-46.

McNamara, C. (1998). *Basic guide to program evaluation.* Retrieved online at http://www.managementhelp.org/evaluatn/fnl_eval.htm

McNeely, M. (2006), *Real-time evaluation strategies.* Presentation at Building State Capacity to Improve Schools: CSR & Title I conference hosted by the U.S. Department of Education, May 11-12, 2006, Atlanta, GA.

Mellard, D. F., & Johnson, E. (2008). *RTI: A practitioner's guide to implementing Response to Intervention.* Thousand Oaks, CA: Corwin Press and Alexandria, VA: National Association of Elementary School Principals.

Mid-continent Research for Education and Learning. (2000). *Evaluation.* Aurora, CO: Author.

Moats, L. C. (2001). When older students can't read. *Educational Leadership* (March 2001), 36-40.

Morrow, L. M. (2005). *Literacy development in the early years: Helping children read and write.* Boston: Allyn & Bacon.

Meyers, E., & Rust, F. O. (2000). The test doesn't tell all: How teachers know that their students are learning. *Education Week* (June 30, 2000), 34, 37.

National Association for the Education of Young Children, and National Association of Early Childhood Specialists in State Departments of Education. (1990). Position statement on guidelines for appropriate curriculum content and assessment in programs serving children ages 3 through 8. *Young Children* 46(3), 21-37.

National Association of Elementary School Principals. (2001). *Leading learning communities: Standards for what principals should know and be able to do.* Alexandria, VA: Author.

National Association of Elementary School Principals. (2008). *Leading learning communities: Standards for what principals should know and be able to do* (2nd Ed.). Alexandria, VA: Author.

National Association of State Directors of Special Education and Council of Administrators of Special Education. (2006). *Response to Intervention: NASDSE and CASE White Paper on RtI.* Retrieved online from http://waccbd.org/RtiResources/RtIAnAdministratorsPerspective1-06.pdf

National Center for Learning Disabilities. (n.d.). *What is Response to Intervention?* Retrieved online from http://www.ncld.org/content/view/1221/398/

National Center for School Engagement. (2005). *How to evaluate your truancy reduction program.* Denver, CO: National Center for School Engagement.

National Early Literacy Panel. (2007). *Synthesizing the scientific research on development of early literacy in young children.* Washington, DC: National Institute for Literacy.

National Research Center on Learning Disabilities. (n.d.). Core findings about response to intervention. *LD InfoZone.* Retrieved online from http://www.ncld.org/content/view/1220/389/

Neide, J. (1996). Supervision of student teachers: Objective observation. *Journal of Physical Education, Recreation & Dance* (September 1996), 14-18.

Niyogi, N.S. (1995). *The intersection of instruction and assessment: The classroom.* Princeton, NJ: Educational Testing Service.

North Carolina Department of Public Instruction. (1999). *Classroom assessment: Linking instruction and assessment.* Raleigh, NC: Author.

North Dakota Department of Public Instruction. (n.d.). *Data based decision making.* Accessed online at http://www.dpi.state.nd.us/speced/personnel/decision.shtm

Northwest Regional Educational Laboratory. (2000). *K-3 Developmental Continuum.* Portland, OR: Author. Retrieved online from www.nwrel.org/assessment/pdfRubrics/k3devcontinuum.PDF.

Olson, L. (2007). Instant read on reading: In the palms of their hands. *Education Week* (May 2, 2007). Retrieved online from http://www.edweek.org/ew/articles/2007/05/02/35form-nm.h26.html?qs=instant%20read

Opitz, M. & Rasinski, T. (1991). *Good-bye round robin.* Portsmouth, NH: Heinemann.

Pajak, E. (2001). Clinical supervision in a standards-based environment: Opportunities and challenges. *Journal of Teacher Education* (May/June 2001), 233-243.

Pardini, P. (2000). Six examples of data-driven decision making at work. *Journal of Staff Development* (Winter 2000). Retrieved online from http://www.nsdc.org/library/publications/jsd/pardini211.cfm

Paris, S. G., & Hoffman, J. V. (2004). Reading assessments in kindergarten through third grade: Findings from the Center for the Improvement of Early Reading Achievement. *The Elementary School Journal 105*(2), 199-217.

Peery, A. (2002). Beyond inservice. *Principal Leadership* (November 2002), 22-28.

Philadelphia Education Fund. (n.d.). *Guidelines for looking at student work.* Retrieved online from www.philaedfund.org/slcweb/guideli.htm

Protheroe, N. (2002). *The role of teacher observation in promoting instructional improvement (ERS Informed Educator).* Arlington, VA: Educational Research Service.

Reeves, D. (2004). Questions and answers from the real world. *Center for Performance Assessment Monthly Email Newsletter* (April 2004). Retrieved online from http://www. makingstandardswork.com/ResourceCtr/enewsletters/enewsletter0404.htm#data

Sanders, J. R., & Sullins, C. D. (2006). *Evaluating school programs: An evaluator's guide.* Thousand Oaks, CA: Corwin Press.

Schilling, S., Carlisle, J., Scott, S., & Zeng, J. (2007). Are fluency measures accurate predictors of reading achievement. *Elementary School Journal* (May 2007), 429-448.

Shellard, E., & Protheroe, N. (2001). *What every principal needs to know about teaching...reading.* Alexandria, VA: National Association of Elementary School Principals and Educational Research Service.

Sparks, D. (2000). Data should be used to select the most results-oriented initiatives: An interview with Mike Schmoker. *Journal of Staff Development* (Winter 2000). Online: www.nsdc.org/ educatorindex.htm

Special Education Division, California Department of Education. (2000). Why children succeed or fail at reading. *The Special EDge* (Autumn 2000), 1 and 6.

Standerfer, L. (2005). Staff development: Finding the right fit. *Principal Leadership* (December 2005), 18.

Stansbury, K. (2001). The role of formative assessment in induction programs. *Reflections* (Spring 2001), 1-2.

Steele, J. L., & Boudett, K. P. (2008). Leadership lessons from schools becoming 'data wise.' *Harvard Education Letter* (January/February 2008).

Steinberg, A. (1998). Reading problems: Is quick recovery possible? *Harvard Education Letter* (September/October 1989). Reprinted in *Reading and Literacy.* Nancy Walser (Ed.). Cambridge, MA: The Harvard Education Letter.

Sugai, G. (2007). *RTI: Reasons, practices, systems, and considerations.* Presentation of the OSEP Center on Positive Behavioral Interventions and Supports.

Thornton, B., & Perreault, G. (2002). Becoming a data-based leader: An introduction. *NASSP Bulletin* (March 2002).

Tierney, R. (1998). Literacy assessment reform: Shifting beliefs, principled possibilities, and emerging practices. *The Reading Teacher* 51, 374-390.

Van der Linde, C. H. (1998). Clinical supervision in teacher evaluation: A pivotal factor in the quality management of education. *Education* (Winter 1998), 328-334.

Van Kraayenoord, C. E., & Paris, S. G. (1996). Story construction from a picture book: An assessment activity for young learners. *Early Childhood Research Quarterly* *11*(1), 41-61.

Vaughn Gross Center for Reading and Language Arts Austin. (2007). Progress monitoring: An essential step in the assessment cycle. *Texas Reading First Quarterly* (October 2007), 2 and 4.

W.K. Kellogg Foundation. (1998). *W.K. Kellogg Foundation evaluation handbook.* Battle Creek, MI: Author.

Wade, H. W. (2001). *Data inquiry and analysis for educational reform* (ERIC Digest 153). Retrieved online from https://scholarsbank.uoregon.edu/dspace/bitstream/1794/3376/1/digest153.pdf

Walker, B. (2008). *Diagnostic teaching of reading.* Upper Saddle River, NJ: Pearson Prentice Hall.

Walser, N. (2007). Response to intervention. *Harvard Education Letter* (January/February 2007). Retrieved online from http://www.edletter.org/insights/response.shtml

Williams, M., Cray, M., Millen, E., & Protheroe, N. (2002). *Essentials for principals: Effective teacher observations.* Alexandria, VA: National Association of Elementary School Principals.

Wilson, E. & Protheroe, N. (2002). *What we know about: Effective early reading instruction.* Arlington, VA: Educational Research Service.

Yap, K., Aldersebaes, I., Railsback, J., Shaughnessy, J., & Speth, T. (2000). *Evaluating whole-school reform efforts: A guide for district and school staff.* Portland, OR: Northwest Regional Educational Laboratory.

# Index